The MILLDALE Story

Its People, its Mission,
its
GOD

Foreword by Bill Stafford

RON OWENS
with
JUDY SCOGGINS

What some are saying about the book

In Psalm 73, a Psalm of Asaph, the end of the wicked is contrasted with that of the righteous. The Psalm concludes with the incredibly potent words, *"But as for me, the nearness of God is my good; I have made the Lord God my refuge, that I may tell of all His works"* (NASB). If I were to list every benefit and blessing that has come to me as a believer in Jesus Christ, I would be terribly hard-pressed to find anything in my entire lifetime more wonderful than the nearness of God. The nearness of God is the very essence of revival. This same nearness of God is at the heart of *The Milldale Story*. The Lord Himself has enabled Ron Owens to capture this precious truth and to set it forth as a rare and brilliant jewel in this captivating account of God's grace and mercy. Would to God that innumerable conferences and camp-meetings might spring up across the land where the manifest presence of God is as mightily felt and known as it was at Milldale. This is what the true church waits for and what the world needs to see. —**Richard Owen Roberts**
International Awakening Ministries, Wheaton, Illinois

Your faith will be strengthened by reading Ron Owens' account of *The Milldale Story*. With the kind of sensitivity and insight for which he is so well known, Owens shares the story of Milldale from its inception to the current days. As Owens paints the captivating Milldale picture with his practiced verbal brush, it will become a fresh reality to you. *The Milldale Story* is a gift to those who have attended, and to many others, like me, who have known of Milldale only by "the hearing of the ear." In *The Milldale Story* you will meet ministers, evangelists, gospel musicians and a faithful camp director, each of whom was used mightily of God to provide solid spiritual foundations in an era when there was a famine of faith across the land.   —**Tom Elliff,** *Living in the Word Ministry, Oklahoma City, Oklahoma*

Ron Owens has done a remarkable job in capturing the essence of one of the truly great miracles of our time, a narrative of God's grace and power in response to the faith and obedience of His people. Only eternity will reveal the endless numbers whose lives have been transformed by the Spirit of God through the ministry of Milldale. Standing firmly upon God's Word, this ministry has had the Father's hand on it from the very first service when a praying people saw God turn a storm away from the campground, in spite of forecasts of devastating and violent weather that was about to engulf the entire region. God has "shown up," and His power has been reflected throughout the nearly 50 years of Milldale's unique and remarkable ministry. This book is a must read for every believer!

—**Jimmy Draper,** *President Emeritus,*
LifeWay Christian Resources

Every believer hungers for a time of refreshment from the deep well of God's Holy Spirit. As I read the Milldale Story, my soul experienced the thirst-quenching taste of God at work through a people who will trust Him. I'm impressed by Ron Owens' style of harmonizing the testimonies, the miracles, the teaching and the faith of these spiritual giants who assembled themselves on these 16 acres in southern Louisiana. My prayer is that the *fires of revival* will once again blaze across our land.

—**John L. Yeats,** *Director of Communications, Louisiana Baptist Convention; Recording Secretary of the Southern Baptist Convention*

The Milldale Story will ignite a revival fire in your soul. It is a record of miracles. It speaks of ordinary people who trusted God to do extraordinary things. Read it and you will find your faith enlarged and you will experience a holy glow in your soul.

—**Herb Reavis, Jr.** Senior Pastor
North Jacksonville Baptist Church, Jacksonville, Florida

The pen of Ron Owens has brought to life the story of a man of God, and the work of a ministry that has touched the world. My life was changed through the conferences. The fire of revival that burns fresh in my heart today was ignited at Milldale. My ministry was shaped by men like Manley Beasley, Bill Stafford, Ron Dunn, Sonny Holland and Brother Jimmy. Thank you Ron for taking us on a trip, from where it all began to what is still going on today.

—**Bill Robertson,** *Director of Pastoral Leadership, Louisiana Baptist Convention*

As one having experienced some measure of genuine biblical revival in the Canadian Revival of the early 1970's which still impacts believers today, it is refreshing to read *The Milldale Story*. What a treat to read of something happening so completely removed from superficial Christian experience, and so spiritually authentic that almost seems unreal in today's religious culture. This book is a clarion call to the church to return to the basics of prayer, faith, holiness, repentance, total surrender, the fullness of the Holy Spirit, the power of God over Satan, and revival. Ron Owens has done a masterful job in gathering true life stories of those personally affected through it. I recommend this book for all who carry a concern about the spiritual ineptness of today's evangelical church.

—**Ralph Sutera,** *Canadian Revival Fellowship*

I remember hearing about Milldale in the 60's when my husband, Bob Doom, and I were on the mission field. My parents wrote me in great detail of the joy in "discovering" Milldale. You can imagine, after experiencing revival in Eastern Europe, my father was always looking to find the Spirit of revival again. He found it at Milldale! I can't tell you the blessing it has been for me to read the full story myself, and to be encouraged to believe God for a fresh move of His Spirit.

—**Sheila Stewart Doom,** *eldest daughter of James A. Stewart*

As a part of religious history, this book is excellent. Outsiders like me can't fully grasp all the nuances involved, but those in "the family" will get the message and rejoice.

—Warren Wiersbe
Author, former director of the Back to the Bible Broadcast

Ron Owens has done another wonderful job of putting in print, *The Milldale Story,* a story that has needed to be told, the story of a special place our Lord has chosen to establish and inhabit in a unique and powerful way. Thank God for raising up Jimmy Robertson, and filling his heart with faith to believe God for extraordinary miracles time and time again. May the Lord cause this book to be distributed to a great host of people who will not only rejoice in the memories of days gone by but who will take advantage of experiencing it personally in the days ahead.

—Jon Moore, *Christ Followers Ministry, Ft. Worth, Texas*

This book is a thrilling and inspirational account of how the Lord used humble men to accomplish great things for God through a multi-faceted ministry. Those with a heart for revival will be greatly blessed by learning *from* and *about* these spiritual pioneers. Milldale has been an oasis for the spiritually thirsty, and its streams are still being felt today.

Harold Vaughan, *Christ Life Ministries, Vinton, Virginia*

A 2001 tribute from **Adrian Rogers** on Jimmy's 65th birthday

Bro. Jimmy, I thank God for the vision He has put in your heart, for your expansive spirit, and for your courage in the things that count. As I've watched you over the years, you have never let up, backed up, or shut up when it came to the Gospel. My prayer for you, my precious brother, is that the days ahead will prove to be an ever rising vista of love, grace and service as you march under the blood-stained banner of our Prince and coming King, even the Lord Jesus.

Published by
Innovo Publishing
Collierville, TN 38017
InnovoPublishing.com
1-888-546-2111

Providing Full-Service Publishing Services for
Christian Authors, Artists & Organizations.
Hardbacks, Paperbacks, eBooks, Audiobooks, Music & Film

Copyright © 2011, 2016 Milldale Baptist Church
All rights reserved.

Printed in the United States of America
U.S. Printing History
First Edition: 2011
Second Edition: August 2016

Cover design by Dennis Davidson

ISBN: 978-1-61314-347-6
Library of Congress Control Number: 2010943118

Unless otherwise identified, all Scripture quotations are taken from
the *King James Version* (KJV).

Other versions used include:

New American Standard Bible (NASB), Copyright © 1960, 1962, 1963,
1968, 1971, 1972, 1973, 1975, 1977, 1995 by The Lockman Foundation.
Used by permission.

New King James Version (NKJV). Copyright © 1982 by Thomas Nelson,
Inc. Used by permission. All rights reserved.

Table of Contents

Cypress History 11

Acknowledgements 14

Foreword by Bill Stafford 15

Introduction 18

Section One: "There was a man..." 21

Chapter 1: Passing the Torch 22

Chapter 2: Son of Tickfaw 26

Chapter 3: Glimpses of Glory 33

Chapter 4: God's Plan Unfolds 41

Chapter 5: The Church God Will Use 47

Chapter 6: The Preacher, a Place, and a People 53

Section Two: A Tree is Planted 57

Chapter 7: A Church is Born 58

Chapter 8: A Branch Begins to Grow: The Camp Meeting 64

Chapter 9: The Camp Meeting Branch Keeps Growing 72

Chapter 10: Teen Camps 78

Chapter 11: A Scotsman Arrives 83

Section Three: Milldale International Ministries 89

Chapter 12: The Greatest Task 90

Chapter 13: The Tree Expands: Printing the Word 102

Chapter 14: "Send forth Thy light:" Distributing the Word .. 109

Chapter 15: Anyway, Anytime, Anywhere 114

Chapter 16: "…and He gave some evangelists…" 118

Chapter 17: "…and He gave some pastors-teachers…" 123

Section Four: Revival and Faith 137

Chapter 18: Where does Revival Begin? 138

Chapter 19: Fires of Revival 148

Chapter 20: What is Faith? (part one) 153

Chapter 21: What is Faith? (part two) 161

Chapter 22: A Prince Has Been Taken From Among Us 169

Interlude: Giants Walked These Grounds 175

Section Five: No Turning Back 187

Chapter 23: Take the Land! 188

Chapter 24: Pressing On 199

Chapter 25: Danny Greig Looks Back 201

Chapter 26: Each Step of the Way 204

Chapter 27: Opportunities for Growth 211

Chapter 28: God's "still small voice" Gets Louder 215

Chapter 29: Through Tragedy to Victory 222

Epilogue 226

Appendix One: Milldale Wives 227

Appendix Two: In Their Own Words 242

Index of Sermons 253

Index of Testimonies 253

Milldale Camp Meeting Preachers 254

Photo Gallery 255

Contact Information 266

The Bald Cypress

The **Bald Cypress** has been chosen as a symbol for this book—a symbol of God's activity for almost half a century on the grounds of Milldale, and to the regions beyond. The land was purchased and the ministry planted in 1963, the same year the Louisiana legislature voted to make the Bald Cypress the State tree. Symbolically, the Milldale ministry, once planted, began to grow like a Cypress, extending its branches to the "four-corners" of the earth.

Cypress History

• The Gopherwood God told Noah to use for the building of the Ark in Genesis 6:14, is generally thought to be Cypress. It is a hardwood known for its durability and resistance to decay. *Milldale has been a place of refuge where many have sought and found shelter from the storms of life. Over the years it has resisted and defeated the efforts of the enemy to cause decay and destroy what God initiated in 1963.*

• The Cypress is known for its **longevity.** The oldest living tree of any kind is thought to be the Cypress found in Soma, Italy. It supposedly was planted in the year of our Lord's birth. The trunk has a circumference of 23 feet. Interestingly, recent **DNA** analysis has shown the Redwood Tree (Sequoias) to be part of the Cypress family. Redwoods are known to live for many years. *"Your throne, oh God, is forever and forever"* (Hebrews 1:8 NKJV).

• **Knees—unique to the Bald Cypress are its "knees."** These are woody projections that surface above the ground or water, sometimes extending as far away as twenty feet from the trunk. These "knees" are part of the root system which some scientists believe help provide oxygen to the tree. Another "knee" function is that of structural support and stabilization. The intertwined root system allows the Bald Cypress to resist very strong winds—even hurricanes rarely overturn them. *"When the whirlwind passes by, the wicked is no more, but the righteous has an **everlasting foundation**"* (Proverbs 10:25 NKJV). This serves as a beautiful analogy for the importance of "knee-time" for Christians during which we receive the spiritual oxygen that is necessary to maintain healthy, spiritual lungs, while developing an intertwining root system with fellow believers that will hold fast in the midst of the strongest winds hurled at us by the enemy.

• Most cemeteries in the East are thickly planted with Cypress trees because the Cypress has traditionally been considered to be both the tree of ***bodily death and the tree of spiritual immortality***. What a picture of a Believer's grave! *"O death, where is thy sting? O grave, where is thy victory?"* (1 Corinthians 15:55).

• The Queen of Sheba moved her empire from the Southern Arabian Peninsula, across the Red Sea to Ethiopia where the Cypress was known as the Thyia, named after the Thyia region where the church at Thyiatira was located (Rev. 1:22 and 2:18). The Cypress was considered the guardian of human civilization, known as the ***Tree of Life, for the Healing of the Nations.***

    This is interesting in light of the references to Eden's ***tree of life*** found in Genesis 3:22-24; the ***tree of life*** of Proverbs 11:30a, *"The fruit of the righteous is a **tree of life**..."* and what John saw in Revelation 22:2—the ***tree of life*** whose fruit is for the ***healing of the nations.*** *"On either side of the river was the **tree of life**, which bore twelve fruits, each tree yielding its fruit every month. **The leaves of the tree were for the healing of the nations**"* (NKJV).

• **Medicinal benefits**—Through the ages the Cypress was found to contain numerous healing properties. For example, the leaves would be crushed, heated, and used as poultices for exterior applications on the body. Sometimes the leaves were crushed and heated, and the oil vapors inhaled by patients with lung problems. This aroma was considered to be so effective that Oriental physicians would send their patients all the way to the Isle of Crete where there were large Cypress orchards.

Another medicinal benefit was discovered in its resin which was used in the treatment of flesh wounds. The Phoenicians found that it served very much like the product we know today as, "New Skin." Additionally, it was discovered that the Cypress wood contains a marvelous anti-viral and anti-bacterial property that the inhabitants of Australia, Africa and India used in the treatment of many ailments. The Cypress is considered to be one of the most important plants in human history.

This all serves as a picture of those who have arrived at Milldale in pain and brokenness over the years, having had the breath knocked out of them by the enemy of their souls, but who, encountering the *Healer of their hearts*, return home refreshed and revived just like the righteous man described in Psalm 1:3. *"He shall be like a tree planted by the rivers of water, that brings forth its fruit in its season, whose leaf also shall not wither; and whatsoever he does shall prosper"* (NKJV). The Cypress thrives best in or next to water!

Note:

Interestingly, the Louisiana Baptist Convention incorporates the Bald Cypress in its logo, along with the Scripture, *"The fruit of the righteous <u>is a tree of life</u>, and he who wins souls is wise"* (Proverbs 11:30).

Acknowledgements

To transfer the activity of God from experience to words on paper is a challenging assignment if your purpose is to present, not just facts, but the heart and spirit of a ministry. Information without divine illumination misses the mark.

For this reason I am so grateful to have been able to work with Judy Scoggins, who not only helped compile the contents of this story, but who has experienced firsthand so much of what you will be reading about in this book. Thank you, Judy!

And a special thanks to:

• Jimmy Robertson and Danny Greig for allowing me the privilege of partnering in the writing of the Milldale Story.

• those who have contributed their own personal stories of how God has used Milldale in their lives, and to those whose testimonies are not included due to space restrictions.

• Bro. Bill Stafford who, from personal experiences, so well encapsulated the spirit and ministry of Milldale in his Foreword.

• my wife, Patricia, who patiently listened, read, and critiqued throughout the writing of *The Milldale Story*.

• those who graciously took the time to read the manuscript and write their responses.

• all those who have been praying that this account of God's activity will challenge, convict and birth hope in the hearts of the readers to reach out in faith, to believe that the God who raised up a "Milldale" can, and will, use them and their churches to impact their generation.

Foreword

When I was asked to write about my relationship to the Milldale Bible Conference in Zachary Louisiana, I felt honored to be able to share the joy I have had in being a small part of such a great ministry. It is impossible, however, for me to write about those years without first relating the events that preceded my initial visit.

In the late 1960's Manley Beasley came to preach a revival meeting for us at Lupton Drive Baptist Church in Chattanooga, Tennessee, where I was pastor. Little did I know that God had sent Manley so that I, personally, could be revived from a ministry of trying, instead of trusting. Manley preached on faith and for six nights I crawled to the mourner's bench in deep contrition. This was my day of awakening to the sufficiency of God and death to my own ability. It was during this week of services that the Holy Spirit confronted me with my need of personal revival, and as I responded in repentance and brokenness, a new awakening to the Wonder of Wonders and to God's desire to take over my life led me to a point of desperation for a Spirit-filled ministry.

That same year, 1968, Manley invited me to go with him to the Milldale Labor Day Conference. That was the beginning of a fresh passion to walk with God in a new dimension. During that week I met Jimmy and Frances Robertson, I heard Hyman Appleman, Duncan Campbell, James Alexander Stewart, Joe Parsons, Manley Beasley, and Sonny Holland, who not only preached but sang the stars down. These men had a tremendous impact on my life, and I left Milldale with an even greater hunger for real revival and a longing to have a personal, intimate walk with a Holy God.

A few years later, in 1972, Jimmy Robertson invited me to return to Milldale to preach at their February conference. I gladly agreed, even though I was overwhelmed by the opportunity. Due to a previous appointment on Monday evening, however, I could not get there until Tuesday morning; and by the time I arrived, the weather had turned very cold and the crowd was small, so they moved the service to a smaller chapel.

I had just had an encounter with God that had led to a fresh new relationship of trust, and before that Tuesday night service Jimmy and I prayed and believed God for a divine manifestation of His presence and power, even though circumstances looked impossible. Little did I know that this was the place where the Lord would demonstrate Himself in such glory that none of us would ever be the same again.

On Friday evening the atmosphere was permeated with an awareness of God's presence. Even as I preached I experienced the touch of God on me. When I gave the invitation people responded in brokenness and repentance, with some being saved and others confessing sins of the flesh. Still others responded in giving miraculously as the Spirit of God moved. Little did I know that this was God's divine appointment that would give me a fresh understanding that the response to my ministry has nothing to do with my performance, but everything to do with His ability and power demonstrated through my mortal flesh.

It has been at Milldale that many of us have been confronted over the years with the truth about faith, repentance, brokenness, self-life, covetousness, temper and jealousy—things that have to be dealt with on a daily basis. We've realized that we're just earthen vessels indwelt by the living Christ.

Probably nothing has brought us to a sense of a personal need for revival more than the sudden awareness that the way up is down; the way out of the storm is through it; the way to be saved is to acknowledge that we're lost, and the way to get is to give. We must die to live; strength comes out of weakness, and desperation is the way to His supply.

In my opinion, no other ministry has impacted more men of God than the revival conferences at Milldale. They have brought thousands to the awareness of humility, godliness, faithfulness and a passion for souls. The fellowship around the meals, the after-service prayer meetings, people walking the grounds day and night interceding for God to intervene in power and glory, all are a part of the Milldale experience. Nothing has impacted my life and ministry anymore than having the privilege to be a part of Milldale Bible Conferences.

Bro. Jimmy went through a very serious illness before a conference where I was scheduled to speak. Even though the doctors gave him no real hope, Jimmy and Frances got a word from God, and they confessed that he would be raised up in time to attend the conference. And he was there! His presence and testimony set the pace for a time of learning to trust God, no matter what you touch, taste, smell, see, or hear. Get a word from God, step out in faith, and act as though it is so 'till God makes it so.

Only eternity will reveal what I have seen, learned and believed by faith as I have preached at this great Revival Center. Though my life and ministry may now be in their twilight years, the memories of Milldale and my association with Jimmy Robertson and all those associated with him, keep me re-fired as I finish the course with fresh vision, passion and direction. Praise God and the Lamb, forever!

—**Bill Stafford,** Evangelist,
Chattanooga, Tennessee

Introduction

11950 Milldale Road—just an address to thousands who have driven along that winding 10-mile stretch of two-lane country road between Highway 409 and Peairs Road. To others, however, this address represents a corner of earth where heaven came down and transformed 16 acres of undeveloped land into a "place of meeting" for thousands of hungry, thirsty souls.

"Can anything good come out of Nazareth?" was the question Nathaniel asked when Philip told him about Jesus. For the uninitiated to God's agenda, the same might be said of those 16 acres, five miles east of Zachary, Louisiana. But the ways of God are not discerned by natural man, and what might look like nothing more than ground and buildings is recorded in the annuls of heaven as an address God has chosen to visit.

• A Dutch Reform Church in New York City was just one of the many struggling, dying American churches in 1857, until God chose one of its upstairs' rooms to house the beginning of a prayer movement that eventually would sweep the east coast, then turn west across the Continental Divide to the Pacific—a movement known as the *Third Great Awakening* that is estimated to have added, in one year, over a million names to the *Lamb's Book of Life*.

• A haystack on Sloan's Meadow in Williamstown, Massachusetts, was just a haystack until it sheltered five William's College students from a thunderstorm, providing them a place to continue their praying for direction from God regarding foreign missionary service. From their deliberations and prayers that day, the *American Board of Commissioners for Foreign Missions* (ABCFM) would eventually be formed, and among the first five missionaries to be sent to India in 1812, were Adoniram Judson and Luther Rice.

And while the haystack prayer meeting missionaries were readying themselves to sail to India, President James Madison, supported by a joint resolution of Congress, was issuing a call to the entire nation to observe a day of humiliation and prayer *"to seek God's merciful forgiveness and His assistance in the great duties of repentance..."*

Perhaps, not coincidently, for our story at least, this year of 1812 was the very year the southern tip of what is known as the *Louisiana Purchase*[1], became the 18th State of the Union, nine years after President Thomas Jefferson had negotiated the acquisition of 900,000 square miles of territory from the French for less than four cents an acre. Louisiana, with its capital, Baton Rouge,[2] would then, 150 years later, be the area where God would begin a stirring in the heart of Jimmy Robertson, a stirring that would lead him to purchase a piece of land in the "boonies" of East Baton Rouge Parish.

The year of the *Milldale Purchase* was 1963,[3] and though miniscule in comparison to the 900,000 square miles of the *Louisiana Purchase,* in God's economy, what was just a small parcel of land was destined to become the launching pad for a

---

[1] **The Louisiana Purchase** stretched from the Gulf coast of Louisiana to the Rockies on the Canadian border.

[2] **Baton Rouge** in French, *Red Stick* in English, or *Istrouma* in the local Indian dialect, was discovered by French Explorer, d'Iberville. The name refers to a tall **Cypress tree** which, after being stripped of its bark, turned red by the blood of freshly killed animals that were wrapped around its trunk. This particular Cypress marked the boundary between the hunting grounds of two Indian tribes.

[3] **1963—a year to remember:** The US Supreme Court's 8-1 decision on June 27 declaring school-sponsored Bible reading in public schools to be unconstitutional; the death of C. S. Lewis and the assassination of President John F. Kennedy on the same day (11/22); Martin Luther King's *"I have a Dream,"* speech from the steps of the Lincoln Memorial; zip codes were introduced; John Glenn orbited the earth; the crime rate soared to 9 times that of the 1950's.

world-wide mission and literature outreach that would touch the "four corners" of the globe.

Yet, this is not only the story of a ministry, it is the story of God's activity in the life of a Louisiana preacher, known by those who know and love him as Bro. Jimmy. In a day when many seek the limelight, at a time when we equate popularity with greatness, it is encouraging to know one who seeks neither.

A. W. Tozer, in the August 12 reading in his daily devotional, *Renewed Day by Day*,[4] says:

"Christians have fallen into the habit of accepting the noisiest and most notorious among them as the best and the greatest. They too have learned (from the world) to equate popularity with excellence. In open defiance of the Sermon on the Mount, they have given their approval, not to the meek, but to the self-assured; not to the pure in heart who see God, but to the publicity hunter who seeks headlines."

This is the story of a place, a person, and a people, who have not sought the accolades of man, but the approbation of the One they serve, for after all,

It matters not if the world has heard, or approves or understands—
The only applause we're meant to seek, is the applause of nail-scarred hands.

This is The Milldale Story.

---

[4] A. W. Tozer, *Renewed Day by Day*, compiled by G. B. Smith, Christian Publications, Inc. (out of print)

Section One

"There was a man…"

"But whatever things were gain to me, those things I have counted as loss for the sake of Christ. More than that, I count all things to be loss in view of the surpassing value of knowing Christ Jesus my Lord…" (Philippians 3: 7-8a, NASB).

1

Passing the Torch

It was after much prayer that Jimmy Robertson stood before the Milldale Baptist Church congregation on that May, 2004, Sunday morning, to announce that it was time for him to begin *passing the torch* to the next generation of runners who would faithfully carry the *light of truth* to their generation.

*The term, **"passing the torch,"** finds its roots in the torch relay that originated in ancient Greece, seven centuries before the birth of Christ. The Apostle Paul would have known about this "sport" through his travels in that part of the world, though, in his symbolic use of "running the race," he did not directly refer to torches. The fire of the torch, nevertheless, is a beautiful picture of the light that we, as Ambassadors of Christ, are carrying.*

In ancient Greece, fire symbolized the creation of the world, renewal and light. At the centre of every city-state there was an altar with an ever-burning fire, and in every home a "sacred flame" burned. Theirs, however, was a false, superstitious fire. **Ours is the Flame of Pentecost.**

What Bro. Jimmy shared that morning was not an announcement of his retirement, it was rather, the beginning of his shifting the load of responsibility to those whom God was raising up to run the next lap.

There was a man...

Milldale Baptist Church

May 30, 2004

Dear Church Family:
In August, 1963, my wife and I, with our three children, began the Milldale Journey, so first, let me express appreciation for the people who were such an inspiration and encouragement to me when I began this ministry. That includes every charter member of the church who helped me start, and every person that the Lord has added to the church since that day. Some came for a little while and left. Some stayed for the long haul. Some stayed for many years and helped, but God used them all in a special way, and there's a love and appreciation in my heart for everyone who's ever passed through Milldale Baptist Church.

It was a great day *when the Lord added Ivan and Jackie Carlson to our church. They've been a constant encouragement to me. Bro. Clinton and Viola Lee have faithfully served on the staff and been an inspiration to my life. I've been privileged to serve with some wonderful secretaries: Jackie, Juanita, Betty, Gloria, and now, Judy. I am indebted to all who are members of this Church and to those who have been members through the years. "Thank you for your love and support."*

It's been a great joy *these last three years to serve with Bro. Ken Fryer and Ramona. I can truthfully say they've won a special place in my heart. I love you Ken and Ramona.*

I also want to express my appreciation to my brother Louis and his wife, Ginny. I became their pastor when they were teenagers at Bluff Creek Baptist Church. They have loved me and served under my ministry for 41 years here at Milldale, driving 100 miles every Sunday to do so. Thank you for this.

This journey has led us into a church ministry that has touched the world with the gospel of Jesus Christ. *Nearly one billion people were reached through the literature ministry* *alone. Millions of pieces of literature are still circulating around the world. For 25 years or more, Ivan faithfully served as manager of the Milldale International Ministries.*

Bro. Sonny has faithfully served God for 40 years in and through our church, *and has been a vital part of our ministry. He has been a friend that has stuck closer than a brother. We've been through many a valley, and we've shouted on many a mountaintop together. We have gone through many endeavors together. Sonny has reached every continent in the world with the gospel. He's preached in over 1,000 churches in America and now has a great ministry in Nicaragua.*

We've had opportunity to have a part in the lives of some of the greatest young preachers in America and have ordained a number of them in this church: *Jason Robertson, Philip Robertson, and others. They are the pride and joy of my life. We had a great influence on Dan Spencer when he came here for years to help with Teen Camps. He would testify today that this is where God gave him roots. Many others have been ordained in our church, and we thank God for all of them: Rusty Bowser, Daniel Fuller, Tim Galipeau, and others.*

We've reached thousands of people through Milldale Bible Conferences from every state in the union. *Hundreds of preachers and missionaries are in pulpits and on the mission field who have made decisions here at Milldale.*

Through the ministry of Fires of Revival, *we have reached every church in the Southern Baptist Convention, encouraging pastors and churches to a ministry of prayer, faith, and revival. Only eternity will reveal what has been accomplished through this church because of your prayers and your labor.*

For nearly 41 years now, Milldale Baptist Church and ministries have been my life, *but the time has come for me to offer my resignation, and for you to love and support a new pastor. I will continue to love this church and serve it under the authority of our new pastor until God calls me home. I will continue to direct the camps. God's given me a new vision and* burden. He's given me renewed faith. He's enlarged my heart to believe Him for more than I've ever believed for in the past.

It will be a new day in the Milldale Camp ministry, I assure you of that. Hundreds will come. God will meet the need and you'll see people's lives changed in the days ahead. I will continue to direct the camps and do itinerant preaching in other churches. I say it humbly, but I believe the Lord has given me a message on faith and prayer and revival and worship that I need to preach and that needs to be heard.

No man has ever enjoyed the ministry and the pastorate of a church more than I have. No pastor's wife has ever loved and appreciated this church more than Frances. I want to publicly thank her for being such a wonderful support over the 48 years we've served in ministry together. The Lord couldn't have given me a better wife. I have so many wonderful memories. Every one of you will always be special to me. You have loved me and my family, prayed for me and given me absolute liberty to obey God. Thank you. You've never handcuffed me. You gave me the liberty to do what God asked me to do. I've made mistakes, but you've loved me in spite of them. I would correct my mistakes and you would go on with me as though I'd never made one. I want to say "Thank you for that!" That hasn't gone unnoticed. Finally, I'm grateful that I am able to leave this church debt free, with all the bills paid!

Today, I'm submitting my resignation, effective May 31, 2004. I request that there be no "goodbye parties" and no gifts. I want us to turn our focus to the new pastor and bestow upon him the same love that you have bestowed upon me. Pray for me, as this will be a great transition in my own life.

I love you,

Jimmy Robertson

The Milldale Story

2

Son of Tickfaw

<u>*Tickfaw, Louisiana:*</u> *located on the Tickfaw River in Tangipahoa Parish. Founded in 1869. Total land area: 1.6 square miles. Present population: 617. Birthplace of Jimmy Robertson, one of 10 children born to Ray and Edna Robertson.*

While writing a story about a small town, a newspaper reporter came across an elderly gentleman sitting in front of the country store, whittling on a stick. *"Have any great men been born here?"* he asked. *"Nope,"* replied the ole-timer, *"Jus' babies!"*

Call to salvation

"It is difficult for me to comprehend how time could have passed so quickly since I first heard the Lord's call. I am very much aware that my life and ministry began in the mind and heart of God, and I can still clearly remember the evening it all started.

"My family didn't attend church back in those days because of the hard work and long hours required to keep our dairy farm going. Cows had to be milked twice a day, and in my younger years, it was all done by hand—the hands of my brothers and sisters and me, for the most part. In those days the farm chores came first, and everything else, even school attendance, took second place.

"I remember when I was fourteen that my Dad, Ray Robertson, decided to take all of us to a revival meeting that was being held not too far from where we lived. It was there that I heard the simple gospel message for the first time. I heard that Jesus died on the cross for my sins; that He was buried and that He rose the third day victorious over sin and death.

"I was deeply convicted of sin and in a few days I found myself behind the barn crying out to God for mercy and salvation. The next Sunday morning I walked a mile and a half to catch a church bus so I could publically confess my faith in Christ. The following Sunday I made the same trek back to the church to be baptized.

"From then, until I was seventeen years old, I had no transportation to get to church, but I had the deep conviction that God had done a work in my life and a growing desire to serve Him burned in my heart. It was a happy day when I was finally able to buy my first car, and it was not long before I began attending Zion Hill Baptist church where J. W. Taylor was pastor. It was there that I met one of the most friendly and loving groups of people I've ever known. On my first visit they became like family to me.

"I was soon going to the Wednesday night prayer meetings, and after one of these services, to my utter amazement, Pastor Taylor invited me to his home for coffee. Me, of all people. What a dear man of God. This simple pastor of a country church took interest in a teenage boy and he began mentoring me. But not only that, he visited my family and it was not long before all the Robertsons were in church. J. W. Taylor was the greatest pastor anyone could have!"

Call to preach

By the time Jimmy was eighteen he had surrendered to preach the gospel, and in spite of what people thought, God enabled him to overcome the inhibitions that he had had about getting up in front of people to speak. Of all the kids in Independence High School, Jimmy Robertson would have been the least expected to have ever succeeded in anything that had to do with public speaking.

Frances Robertson recalls those days when her future husband took an "F" in English class rather than going through the ordeal of giving an oral report.

"Jimmy graduated two years before I did. We lived in a predominantly Catholic community and there were few Baptists teaching in our school. One of those exceptions, however, was Mr. Hover, who taught English. When he heard that Jimmy had surrendered to preach he told me,

'There is no way that that boy will ever preach, because he is so shy.'

"He reminded me of the 'F' Jimmy had taken, rather than having to get up in front of the class.

"Later, when I told Mr. Hover that Jimmy was now doing a lot of revival preaching, he told me that he'd like to go and hear him. I gave him Jimmy's schedule and one weekend, when a meeting was in the area, Mr. Hover was in the audience.

"The following week, the English teacher who said Jimmy would never preach, found me and said:

'This is not the Jimmy Robertson I taught. I can't believe what I've seen and heard.'"

Taking to the street

God began to open doors of ministry such as Sunday pulpit supplies and revival meetings. From the beginning Jimmy had a burden to see people saved, so he didn't wait around for invitations to preach like he saw some doing. He believed the field was the world and the call he had received to preach was from God, so he began preaching in every place he had the opportunity.

"I started a street ministry on the Saturdays when I didn't have a church meeting scheduled" recalls Jimmy. "In those days you could use sound systems, so I got me a public address

There was a man...

system, the one with the horn on top. That old horn could be heard a mile away!

"I started going to Hammond, Louisiana, where I would preach mid-morning on Saturday, then I would go on to Amite. In the afternoon I would head for Natalbany where there was a large grocery store surrounded by trees. It had a porch across the front and lots of tables and chairs. All kinds of people, including migrant workers, who had come to pick strawberries, would gather there every Saturday afternoon. I saw this as a great opportunity to preach the gospel.

"God mightily worked among those folk, as well as in Hammond and Amite. Many times people would step out of the crowd, walk forward, kneel down and make public professions of faith in the Lord Jesus Christ. Backsliders were being reclaimed, and it was amazing what God was doing right out on the streets. What we saw happen back then was probably more than you see happening in many churches today."

The Tent of Meeting

In Exodus 33:7, we read, *"Now Moses used to take the tent and pitch it outside the camp, far off from the camp, and he called it the tent of meeting. And everyone who sought the Lord would go out to the tent of meeting which was outside the camp."* It was to this tent that Moses and the people would go to meet God.

Using a tent for revival services may sound a bit archaic to some of our readers, but there was a day when tents were used by many evangelists for their meetings. It was in tent meetings that thousands of souls were transferred by the Holy Spirit from the Kingdom of Darkness to the Kingdom of Light. And so it was that Jimmy Robertson, at the age of 18, made a step of

The Milldale Story

faith, and with the help of his family he purchased a 40 x 80 foot tent that would seat up to 400.

The first place he and his brothers set the tent up was in a field behind Tom Hilton's café, in Hineston, Louisiana, where God so blessed that before they had finished that meeting, they'd received an invitation to hold a crusade in West Monroe. Up went the tent again on Monday, and Jimmy started preaching that night.

"And my, how God blessed," remembers Jimmy. "People were being moved by the Spirit of God; lives were being changed, and then, on Friday night, things really began to get exciting.

"A woman had come forward earlier in the week to ask us to pray for her son who had just been released from prison, after having served 20 years for murder. God placed a heavy burden on my heart for this young man, and I began to fast and pray that God would draw him to the meeting and save him.

"Well, on Friday night, unknown to me, that man was sitting on the back row, and as soon as I gave the invitation he was the first to come down the aisle. He told me his story of being guilty of murder, of serving time in the penitentiary, and how he had lived a vile, wicked life. He asked me if I thought God could save him, and I told him I certainly did. He said:

'I heard you preach on the grace and mercy of God and I wonder if there is grace and mercy for me.'

"That night, this convicted murderer repented of his sin and turned his life over to Jesus. He then got up off his knees and shared his testimony with the congregation about what God had just done for him, right there at the altar.

"His mother, who was sitting near the back of the tent, started to shout and came running down the aisle. She ran across the front of the tent, then back up the other side to her seat. It was the first time I had ever seen shouting in a Baptist meeting. I decided right then and there that I liked it!

"When this man had finished giving his testimony, a woman came broken and weeping to the altar.

'Preacher,' she said, *'I've been a prostitute, drug addict and there is nothing that I have not done. I am a guilty, vile, wicked sinner. Do you think that God would have mercy on a person like me? If he can forgive a murderer like that man, He can probably save me.'* I looked at her and said:

'Ma'am, you are the kind of person that the Lord Jesus died for.'

"She knelt at the altar, gave her heart to Christ, and then she also shared her testimony with the congregation. You should have seen the ladies in that tent coming down to put their arms around her. I have never seen such love expressed to anyone. Here was a harlot, a vile, sinful woman whom God had saved, now standing before us as white as snow.

"As a result of what happened on that Friday night, the word spread and people began coming from far and near. Many more got saved, while others rededicated their lives. As a result of what God did, decisions continued to be made for weeks to come in the church that had sponsored the tent-meeting.

"During those days there was a sense of an unusual anointing of the Holy Spirit that resulted in a deep conviction and brokenness in the hearts of the people. That is something that we have lost in our day. You seldom see real conviction anymore, where folk are broken and weep over sin."

Power through prayer

Jimmy began taking the tent to small communities all across their local area. Sometimes they would invite other preachers to hold services. They saw many people saved during those days and, as Bro. Jimmy recalls, one of the main contributing factors to what they were seeing was the prayer meeting they always held in the tent following each service.

"I remember people praying and seeking God's face for revival for two and three hours after the service," recalls Jimmy. *"Sometimes, when we were near enough to one of our own homes, we would go there to pray as well. Those were times when we experienced the **glory of God** in our midst as we prayed. I firmly believe that the supernatural work we saw happening in the lives of so many who attended the meetings was largely due to the time that we spent on our knees."*

Not only were there the tent revivals, but Jimmy was also receiving more and more invitations to preach in churches. He preached over twenty "revivals" the first year of his ministry. *"How and why God would ever open such doors to a man like me, I will never be able to explain,"* says Bro. Jimmy. *"But nevertheless He did, and as a result I have tried to walk with an open heart before Him ever since."*

A testimony—Philip Robertson[5]

"One of the things about my Uncle Jimmy that has had a profound impact on me over the years is his personal prayer life. I actually lived with him and Aunt Frances on weekends and during the summers when I was attending New Orleans Seminary. I can remember the nights when I was awakened in the wee hours of the morning by his agonizing in prayer in the next room. I would slip out in the hall, peek in the door, and see him on his knees, or his face, interceding for others. That had a huge impact on me! I saw him "in the secret place," not just in the pulpit. It proved to me that his faith, his relationship with the Lord, and his prayer life were the real thing."

---

[5] Pastor of the Philadelphia Baptist Church, Deville, Louisiana. See chapter 15 for complete testimony.

3

Glimpses of Glory

"Once you've been baptized in the fire, you can never again be satisfied with smoke"—Jimmy Robertson

Immediately following Solomon's prayer of dedication for the Temple, we read; *"Fire came down and consumed the burnt offering and the sacrifices, and <u>the glory of the Lord</u> filled the temple"* (2 Chronicles 7:1-3).

The glory of the Lord, simply stated, is the manifest presence of God, and where He reveals Himself there is always a sense of His holiness and power. Here, at this dedication, as was the case with Moses' encounter with God at the burning bush; Elijah, on Mt. Carmel; Isaiah's vision of the Throne; and the Day of Pentecost, God manifested His presence in the form of fire. And where there is fire, there is purging, there is light, there is warmth, and there is power.

"We do not preach ourselves, but Christ Jesus the Lord, and ourselves your bondservants for Jesus sake. For it is the God who commanded light to shine out of darkness, who has shone in our hearts to give the light of **the knowledge of the glory of God in the face of Jesus Christ"** (2 Corinthians 4:5-6 NKJV).

It was God

Jimmy had a meeting scheduled about 3 miles from his home, in a church that had a seating capacity of 125. It was only running between 30 and 40 in attendance at the time, so it was to everyone's surprise that the church was full that first Sunday morning. And God came.

Jimmy remembers such a moving of God's Spirit in brokenness and repentance that, on Monday night, there wasn't room in the sanctuary for all the people who had come, so they got chairs from other areas of the building and lined them up outside, in front of the church, row upon row.

"I stood in the doorway and preached," recalls Jimmy. "The next day we borrowed about 300 more chairs from another church. The people were coming from everywhere. This congregation that had been averaging between 30 and 40 was now running over 300. Revival had begun, and we had only spent about $10 on publicity.

"**It was God** who was doing the work, and **it was God** who was bringing the people out. **It was God** who was changing lives, and **it was God** who was causing such a spirit of brokenness and repentance. **It was God** who was convicting people of their need of a Savior. What a glorious time we had in that little church. I can't help but think of the difference between then and now. In those days the meetings would run way past the regular closing time because people had such a hunger and thirst for God. Now, oh my, how things have changed. Today, very often churches are not willing to hold more than, what they call, a *one day revival*. They're afraid their people won't respond to a series of meetings. **I tell you, God has not changed, and where He is present in His glory, the people will come.**"

GLORY in Alabama

Another real **glimpse of glory** happened in a small town in Alabama where this particular church ran around 200 in attendance. When Jimmy preached on Sunday morning he felt that the people were freezing up on him, and he didn't know why. That afternoon he decided to visit Joe Prather, a pastor friend of his whose church was nearby.

"Joe," he said, *"I'm probably going to be leaving tonight after the service. I feel like the people have rejected the message*

and they've rejected me. There's no use for me to waste my time or their time. I'll probably close out the meeting tonight and go home."

Joe asked what his sermon was about, and when Jimmy told him that he had preached on missions and giving as it applied both to individuals and churches, Joe laughed and said:

"I can tell you what the problem is, preacher. Money and the hoarding of money is their God. They have about $150,000[6] in certificates of deposit (CDs) *in the bank, and they have no plans to use the money on anything but themselves."*

Having learned that the hoarding of money was the god of that church, Jimmy went back to the church and prayed the rest of the afternoon. God spoke to his heart and told him what to do. In the meeting that night, he said:

"We're going to have morning and evening services and I'm going to start preaching on faith in the morning, and I'm going to do the same thing all the way through Friday night. Every message is going to be on faith giving, faith living, sacrifice and missions. And just so you'll know, I'm not going to take a dime from this church. I'm expecting God to do something supernatural, and I don't want you to think that when I talk about giving, and especially giving sacrificially by faith, that I am preaching this for self gain. I know that God will take care of my need so I'm not going to accept one nickel from this church because I'm giving this week as a service of love to you."

Jimmy taught and preached on faith, Monday, Tuesday and Wednesday. Then, on Thursday night, a woman stood up in the service and suggested to the pastor that, since the preacher would not take up an offering for himself, maybe they should still go ahead and take one up for him. Bro. Jimmy told them again that he would not accept any offering and that there was

---

[6] In today's currency $150,000 would be in excess of $400,000

no way in the world that he was going to let this church give him a penny.

With that settled, she asked the pastor if he would allow an offering to be taken for Bro. Harold Brown and the *Fairhaven Children's Home*. Harold had been at that church just a week or two before, so the pastor agreed. He said:

"We need to give the people an opportunity to express what they have heard preached. We need to respond to the Word of God."

The pastor, knowing that Bro. Jimmy was involved with the *Fairhaven Children's Home* ministry, asked:

"How much does it take to run Fairhaven for a month?" *"About $3,000,"* Jimmy said. "That woman then turned to Jimmy and said: *'You have preached on faith all week and now, will you agree to believe God for a $3,000 offering to give to Bro. Harold Brown?'*

"There was nothing for me to do but say *'Yes,'* recalls Jimmy. "After all, that is what I had preached on all week, and it was obvious that God had been moving and speaking to the people. Well, the next day the pastor took me aside and said that they had never received over $400 in any love offering they'd ever taken up at that church, and that most of those offerings were for the needs of the church. He said that they had never had an outsider receive even that large an amount. I said,

"Pastor, you're going to see a miracle tonight. You are going to see a $3,000 offering."

The evidence of things not seen

When the pastor stood to share about the offering that evening, Jimmy turned to his friend, Joe Prather, and said; *"I wish the pastor would have let me take up the offering because he sure isn't doing a very good job of presenting the need."* God immediately rebuked him and he had to turn to Bro. Joe again; *"I'm sorry,"* he said. *"I should have never said that, because I don't want to trust in the arm of flesh. I want to trust the Spirit of God to work and move and perform a miracle in this church tonight so that God will be glorified in the giving."*

The ushers began passing the plates, and when they returned to the front the pastor looked at Jimmy and said:

"*Well, the guessing is over. How much money do you say is in the offering plates?"*

In a voice loud enough for the entire congregation to hear, Jimmy said:

"*I believe there is over $5,000 in the offering."* Turning to the ushers, he said, *"Go and count it right now, and if you come back and say there is less than that, I will say that you and the deacons stole it."*

Naturally, the people laughed as the ushers took the offering back to count it, and it was not long before they returned with a slip of paper which they handed to Bro. Jimmy. He looked at the paper, then at the faces of those people who were about to witness the biggest financial miracle they had ever seen. Holding up the piece of paper, he announced:

"The offering total is $5,150"

Before he could say anything else the people began to stand and praise God. Some were even weeping. The altar filled with people as they began repenting of their unbelief. There was brokenness, and some folk, still in their seats, stood to confess that they had been going to that church for years and never thought that they would ever see anything out of the ordinary— they had never expected to see anything supernatural happen in their church.

There was confession of other sins that had kept folk from following after God. The pastor and Bro. Jimmy just stood back and watched a supernatural manifestation of the Holy Spirit and **glory of God.** Five or six adults were saved that night, and several others joined the church by letter.

The Milldale Story

Faith and half a tank

It was very late by the time Jimmy headed for his car that night, and God still had one more test of faith waiting. Bro. Jimmy will never forget what happened next.

"I had put every penny I had in the offering," he recalls, "and when I got in the car and looked at the gas gauge I realized that I only had half a tank of gas left, which would have gotten me about half way to *Fairhaven Children's Home* in Covington, where I was planning to spend the night. I figured that Harold Brown was not going to mind being awakened in the wee hours of the morning to make me a cup of coffee, in light of the $5,150 check I was going to give him—but I had to get there first.

"As I sat looking at the gas gauge I prayed, *'God I have obeyed you and done what you told me to do when I put all my money in the offering plate. Now, you're going to have to take care of my gas need if I'm going to make it to Covington.'*

"I had no sooner finished praying when there was a tap on the car window. A man was standing there weeping. As I rolled down the window, he said:

'When I got in my car God spoke to me and said I was to give you $20. This is not from the church, it is from me, because God said give it. I don't know why, I just know God said to give you $20.'

"I knew why, of course, but in order to increase this man's faith I told him to look at my gas gauge. I told him that I didn't have a penny in my pocket because I had put all I had in the offering, knowing that God would meet my need if I had a part in meeting the need of the *Fairhaven Children's Home.*

"I got gas, took the check to Bro. Brown, and did we ever have a hallelujah good time right there in the middle of the night. Yes, those were days when we had real **glimpses of God's glory.**"

There was a man...

Glory among Arizona's elite
"I remember going to a church in Arizona where we had another **glimpse of glory.** I had met the pastor on another occasion and knew that he had two doctoral degrees which, I found out, was important to the people in his church. When I arrived on Saturday evening, he said:

'Bro. Jimmy, First Baptist is made up of many elite people. Tomorrow you'll be preaching to college professors, the chief of police, several city council members, and other leaders of the community. They're all members of this church.'

"I went to my room, after eating very little supper, feeling so inadequate. I got on my face before God and prayed most of the night.

'Oh God, I can't, but you can.'

I said, *'Unless there is such a supernatural anointing on me to make the difference, I will be a laughing stock to these people in the morning. Here I am, with little education, speaking to men and women with all kinds of university degrees.'*

I said, *'God you're going to have to do something for me tomorrow.'*

Before I went to sleep God gave me the assurance that He would do it."

No degrees needed...when God is present
"The nearness of God is my good" (Psalm 74:3, NASB).

The next morning Bro. Jimmy, the preacher with no degrees, delivered the message God had put on his heart with *holy boldness,* and when the invitation was given the altar filled from one end to the other. Interestingly, extending an altar call was something they never did in that church, but now, here were men and women crying out to God—the chief of police, some of the college professors, some of the town council were on their faces, weeping before the Lord.

"When the service finally ended," Jimmy recalls, "they asked if we could hold services every morning. We did, and

The Milldale Story

God mightily moved in every meeting. There was conviction of sin and brokenness like that church or town had never experienced before. Some of the very elite in town were coming to Christ. It was one of the most glorious meetings I had been a part of in a long, long time. How exciting to just stand back and watch God, **in His glory,** work supernaturally. I was again convinced that if we would just get out of the way, and **not touch God's glory,** and let Him take over, that He is well able to do exceedingly, abundantly above anything we could ever ask or think."

"A watching world still waits to see what can be done through one who touches not that which is God's alone. Touch not the glory, for it belongs to God."[7]

---

[7] Words by Irma Davison. From the song, *Touch Not the Glory,* by Ron and Patricia Owens

There was a man...

4

God's Plan Unfolds

"For I know the plans I have for you, declares the Lord, plans for welfare and not for calamity to give you a future and a hope. Then you will call upon Me...and I will listen to you. And you will seek Me and find Me, when you search for Me with all your heart."
—Jeremiah 29:11-13 (NASB)

Two become one

Jimmy met Frances Leonard, a beautiful 16 year-old young lady, in his senior year. He was immediately struck with her and they were soon dating, though Frances says those were not actually dates as all Jimmy was doing was taking her, and some of her family, to his preaching engagements. Supposedly, they went along to hear him preach, not because they thought they needed a chaperone. Anyway, back in those days very few people had cars, so Jimmy squeezed as many as he could into his 1954 Chevy and headed off happily to the meetings.

They married as soon as Frances finished high school and she instantly found herself the wife of the pastor of Bluff Creek Baptist Church. Bro. J. W. Taylor's wife, Joyce, was the only pastor's wife Frances had known, and she wanted to be just like her.

Jimmy recalls how Frances loved everyone in the church. She taught Sunday School, spoke to every child and every adult each time there was a service. "We usually were the last ones to leave the church because of Frances' fellowshipping with the people," remembers Jimmy. "As I look back over the fifty plus years of ministering together, I have not known her to have ever had a controversy with a single person. I've always said that in those early days there were occasions when I expect one of the three churches I pastored; Bluff Creek Baptist, Big Island

Baptist in Deville, Louisiana, or Carmel Baptist in Pineville, probably would have fired me if they hadn't loved Frances so much! Many times we would entertain 15-20 church members at a time for a meal and fellowship."

A God-given dissatisfaction

After nine years in the ministry, though outwardly things seemed to be going well, Bro. Jimmy felt himself becoming dissatisfied with what he saw God doing in his own personal life and ministry. As he spent more and more time reading Scripture he realized that his life fell far short of what he saw of New Testament Christianity.

"I was in a meeting at Friendship Baptist Church in Pollock, Louisiana, where my friend, Harold Brown, was pastoring," recalls Jimmy. "As God dealt with my heart there was a longing to make an absolute commitment to Him, but I was afraid that if I totally turned my life over to God that He would ruin me. If I said, *'Anytime. anywhere,'* He would send me to the jungles of Africa, to China, India, or to some obscure place. But as I studied His Word, I came to realize that God wanted His best for me. If I was totally committed to Him, my heart's desire would be to do whatever He wanted me to do. I could know joy and happiness by doing His perfect will. I began to desperately seek the Lord, and soon came to a point of absolute surrender. I experienced a fresh refilling of the Holy Spirit. I'll never forget that day. *I gave up to God.*

"I didn't have an emotional experience but I had the assurance that this burden and vision would ultimately be fulfilled in my life. I desperately wanted God to do something in my life and ministry that would be unexplainable apart from the supernatural activity of God. I was so desperate that I signed a statement in my Bible that I would pay any price and make any sacrifice to see God come in revival to my own life, as well as the life of the church I was pastoring. It was at this point that I began to understand that *Deity honors desperation.*"

There was a man . . .

A dream is planted

The Bluff Creek Baptist Church parsonage Jimmy and Frances were living in was located next to an old Methodist campground. The old-timers in the community would reminisce about how people used to come from all across the South to those camp meetings, and how God mightily worked. Some of the greatest preachers of past generations had ministered on those grounds including the British evangelist, Gypsy Smith.[8] As they related those stories, Jimmy's heart began to burn with a holy fervor to see God do it again.

He began meeting with two preacher friends, Sonny Holland and Jesse Norris, in the old tabernacle on that Methodist campground to pray for guidance for the ministry God was laying on their hearts. God made His presence known in those prayer meetings, and this created an even greater hunger and thirst for Him. As the Psalmist says: *"My soul thirsteth for God, for the living God"* (Psalm 42:2a). Jimmy also discovered that anything God required of him, He would work it out, in and through him.

"Because I had never been to college or seminary," continues Jimmy, "I felt so inadequate, but grateful, because this drove me to absolute dependence upon God. I knew that whatever happened, God would have to do it. He assured me that if I would obey 2 Timothy 2:25, *'Study to show thyself approved unto God, a workman that needeth not to be ashamed, rightly dividing the word of truth,'* that He would take over my life and accomplish His purposes. I rediscovered the truth that Christ not only died for me, but that He lives in me to be everything I will ever need.

---

[8] Gypsy Smith, famous British evangelist (1860-1947). He was born in a Gypsy tent and saved at the age of 16. General William Booth, founder of the Salvation Army, invited him to join him in his evangelistic crusades. He made over 40 preaching trips to America, Australia and South Africa.

The Milldale Story

"I encourage young preacher boys to get all the education they can possibly get, the education that I didn't have the opportunity to have, but whether blessed with formal education or not, we have God's promise in 1 Thessalonians 5:24 that, *'Faithful is he that calleth you, who will also do it.'"*

Jimmy was 19 when he went to pastor Bluff Creek Baptist church. He stayed for 3 years before moving on to Central Louisiana. He had been there but a couple of years, however, when Bluff Creek asked him to consider returning to them. There had been a theological issue with the pastor who had followed Jimmy. After initially refusing to consider it, when they called again, he sensed the Holy Spirit leading him back.

"They were now running from 40 to 50 in attendance," recalls Jimmy, "and not only were their finances down, they were having other problems. The church I had been pastoring in Central Louisiana had just built a new building, and had provided Frances and me a brand new parsonage. We were settling in, and we were comfortable when God said, *'Go,'* so we prayed and God gave us the peace and grace to obey.

What Bro. Jimmy didn't realize at the time was that God was beginning to set in motion a plan, and a ministry, that would one day touch the world. But how could this be? Jimmy Robertson? Bluff Creek Baptist Church? An old Methodist campground? Well,

> *Do two plus two always make four?*
> *No, with our Lord they can make more.*
> *Five little loaves, two fish you say?*
> *Five thousand can't be fed that way.*
> *Five thousand? You just lend an eye*
> *And watch those two fish multiply.*
> *Unlimited what God can do,*
> *Unlimited His work through you!*[9]

---

[9] From the song, *Nothing is Impossible,* by Ron and Patricia Owens

There was a man...

The bonding of hearts.
"We held a revival the first week we returned," remembers Jimmy. "And during that meeting Bro. Sonny Holland and his family joined the church, along with his brothers and a number of other people. We probably added 15 to the church roll that first week. Sonny had already surrendered to preach the gospel of the Lord Jesus, and it was not long before we ordained him to the ministry. We became great friends and began to spend many wonderful times together in prayer and revivals.

"Later, when I invited Bro. Jesse Norris to preach a series of meetings at Bluff Creek, God was already doing an unusual work in my heart. He had been dealing with me about a Camp and Bible Conference ministry. As I shared this burden with Bro. Jesse and Sonny, and as we prayed together, they caught the vision and began bearing the burden with me.

"There was an old Methodist camp ground near the church. We would often go over at night to pray under the old tabernacle pavilion, sometimes until two or three o'clock in the morning. God would show up, move in our hearts, speak to us, and fill us with a fresh spirit of revival every night we were there. Oh the **wonder and glory of God** in those prayer meetings. It is impossible to explain what He was doing in our three lives every time we met. We would pray, and then, the next night back at the church, we'd see the glory of God manifested as lives were transformed and the entire church would be touched by a spirit of revival."

Jimmy began to seriously pursue the idea of the Camp Meeting ministry that God had placed on his heart, so he met with the deacons of the church to share the vision with them. They didn't know what to think. They had never heard of such a thing. Some of them even wondered whether Jimmy was really a Baptist. They told him that they didn't feel a Camp Meeting ministry was for their church, and they used this as an excuse to complain about all the "outsiders" who had joined the church and who were beginning to take over.

The Milldale Story

Providentially, Jimmy already had a "Tent Bible Conference" planned for that August. He told the deacons that since they felt they could not join him in what God was leading him to do, when the meeting was over he would resign and start another church. He told them that he would take with him only the ones who had joined the church since he had come as pastor. He told them that he was not going to take those who were already there, but only those they would probably like to get rid of anyway. He would only take the ones they considered to be "outsiders."

And so it was that God was preparing the way for a move to East Baton Rouge Parish and the purchase of those 16 acres of land out in the country, eight miles east of what was then the "small community" of Zachary, Louisiana.

There was a man . . .

5

The Church God Will Use

"Every church ought to be God's hospital and dining hall. It should be a place where the broken and bruised can find healing. It should be a place where the spiritually hungry and empty can be fed. It should be a place where the lonely find fellowship and the brokenhearted find comfort. It should be a place where the friendless can find friends, the kind who stick closer than a brother."—Bro. Jimmy

A testimony—Charles (Chuck) Sackman[10]
"God led me to go with Sam Moore to the Milldale Labor Day Camp Meeting in 2006, not long after I had become the pastor of Piney Point Baptist Church in Rogers, Arkansas. That weekend changed the course of my ministry forever. I heard men preach the Word of God with such boldness and exhortation that my world literally flipped right-side up.

"Soon after that I began to disciple young men, and in the last four years I've seen God call 26 of them into the preaching ministry. It has been overwhelming. They have become bold proclaimers of the gospel and have planted four new churches in the last two years, with three more in the works.

"Every September I take my preacher boys, some older than myself, to the Labor Day Conference where they are fed and encouraged in the faith. I cannot express how grateful I am to the Lord Jesus for the impact that Milldale has had, and continues to have, on my life and ministry.

---

[10] Pastor, Piney Point Baptist Church, Rogers, Arkansas

A Word from Bro. Jimmy

A fundamental reason why God has been able to use and bless Milldale Baptist Church and its ministries is that the preaching of the Word of God has been preeminent.

In Matthew 24:35, Jesus said: *"Heaven and earth shall pass away but my words shall never pass away."* The kind of church God can use is a "Word-centered" church.

A Word-centered church

If God is to use a church, it must be built on His Word. Ron Dunn once said to me that I would never believe the number of people who ask him why he attended Milldale so often. He said: *"I always tell them it's because the ministry is built on the Word of God."*

There is liberty and praise at Milldale, and it's not built on shallow emotionalism, but on divine revelation when the Word is preached. Before Ron Dunn died, he told me, *"I am so grateful that Milldale never waivered in its belief in the preaching of the Word of God."*

There's no substitution for God's divine revelation. Ultimately, that which is built on truth is the only thing that will be eternal. When I was a young man, my pastor, J. W. Taylor, told me, *"Jimmy, make much of the preaching of the cross."*

Paul said, *"I know nothing among you except Jesus Christ and Him crucified"* (1 Corinthians 2:2). He also said, *"I will glory in the cross"* (Galatians 6:14).

A praying church

In every instance in Scripture, when God gets ready to do a supernatural thing, He burdens His people to pray. Every revival has been birthed in prayer. In Acts we see the pattern of a New Testament church that continued in the Apostle's doctrine and prayer. In every crisis the early church prayed. A church that is not a praying church can have a lot of activity and exhibition of the flesh, but there will be little divine activity. The church that prays can have what God can do. If they are not a praying church, they can only have what man can do which is not much, and it will not last.

I believe the reason there is little revival in the church today is that there are so few prayer warriors. Milldale has always had a group of praying people. Our senior citizens have been the spiritual backbone of the church. They know how to intercede before God. In addition to these, thousands of others across America are praying daily for the Milldale ministry.

When I was a young man I remember there being prayer warriors in the church — people who knew how to engage in spiritual warfare on their knees. Back then, we believed that the victories experienced in the church were the result of victories won in secret. But today, very few churches even have prayer meetings anymore. And very few churches are experiencing revival and the glory of God in their midst. For God to use a church, it must be a church on its knees.

A revived church

There is a difference between revival and evangelism. Revival is when God visits a congregation in a supernatural, sovereign way that changes the hearts of the people and the very atmosphere of a church because, in revival God sanctifies His own and produces holiness. As a result, there will be a burden for souls and a renewed interest in evangelism as you see people gloriously saved. This only comes through prayer.

A giving church

From the beginning, Milldale Baptist Church was taught the great principle of giving by faith from the resources provided by God. Over and over again God vindicated himself through miracle offerings from a handful of humble, praying, people. When an offering was received at Milldale, whether it was for a missionary, an evangelist, or a needy saint, I've never been embarrassed at the response of the church. We believed the great principle of Scripture that says, *"Give and it shall be given to you"* (John 4:14). As the people gave sacrificially, God would supernaturally meet their need, and one of the blessings has been to see how cheerfully our people gave. It was always an exciting day when a special offering was scheduled for the Bible printing ministry, the building program, or for some missionary's need. The folk came prepared to give sacrificially because they had prepared themselves spiritually. There was always an overwhelming joy and a manifestation of God's glory. People worshiped God with their gifts.

A "faith-practicing" church

A church must believe that God will hear and answer the prayer that is prayed in faith and is according to the will of God. Faith is reality. It is the title deed to that which we are asking God for. Manley Beasley used to say, *"Faith is acting like a thing is so when it is not so in order for it to be so because God says it is so."* If you can get a church praying, if you can get a church believing God, things will happen.

A worshiping church

For most people, worship is generally relegated to a Sunday morning service, but the truth is, worship is a lifestyle, and if people haven't worshiped at home, it is doubtful that they will have a worship encounter with God when they get to church. If you want to know how often you worship, ask yourself, *"How many times have I been changed from glory to glory?"* You cannot meet a God in worship without some change happening in your life. We do not need an *imitation* of Jesus, we need the *impartation* of His life into ours in order to bring about that change. When we come to church we need to abandon competing, outside thoughts. There's a time and place for thinking of other things, but not when we approach God in worship. The worth that you put on God will determine the quality of worship you will offer. We worship Him because He is worthy.

True worship always originates in the spirit of man; then it is expressed through emotions and sometimes even through the body. Worship is not something that is worked up on the outside until we get ourselves stirred up. A person can listen to preaching and still not worship. A person can enjoy a great song service and still not worship. A lot of people attend all day singing conventions but never worship God, or experience any real change in their lives.

Now, understand, I have nothing against singing. It has played an important part in worship throughout the Bible and Christian history. True worship that originates in the heart is often expressed outwardly through music. God has blessed Milldale over the years with many great musicians, both in the church and in the camp meetings. One of Milldale's legacies is God-centered worship.

A musician's testimony—Monte Holland
"I count it a privilege to have spent most of my life here at Milldale. Some of my fondest childhood memories include walking hand in hand with Dr. James Stewart as he pointed out the awesomeness of God's creation. The foundation of my Christian life was grounded in my childhood as I watched men of faith, like my Dad (Sonny Holland), Bro. Manley Beasley, Bro. Jimmy Robertson, Bro. Jesse Norris and Bro. Harold Brown as they believed God for miracles to meet their needs. I saw God faithfully answer and show Himself alive and powerful in each situation. I can truly say with the Psalmist, *'I have been young and now am old; yet I have not seen the righteous forsaken nor his seed begging bread'* (Psalm 37:25).

"By His grace, God has allowed me to cross paths with so many wonderful brothers and sisters in Christ through the Camp Meeting ministry. I'll be forever grateful to my Lord for those experiences and the "old landmarks" He has afforded me.

"I count it an honor to work hand in hand with my pastor, Bro. Danny Greig, as Minister of Music at Milldale Baptist Church. We both have seen the undeniable power of God through our own heritage, a heritage that we now desire to pass on to the next generations.

"As many churches today steer away from using the old hymns in their worship, I have a strong desire to bring back the awesome power of praise and worship we find in them.

"There are many new choruses that certainly have their place in today's worship, but nothing moves me more than singing the old hymns of Zion, knowing that they are not just words in a book, but songs that were born out of times when God took old saints and created circumstances that would cause them to *"look full in His wonderful face,"* and simply trust Him to use the circumstances for His glory and honor.

"Hymns like *Great is Thy Faithfulness,* and *It is Well With My Soul*, speak to the very heart of man, and in turn glorify our wonderful Lord. God inhabits the praises of His people through Psalms, hymns and spiritual songs. I believe that the singing of these great hymns of the faith is an important part of worship that should be passed down to our children and grandchildren so that when they face the storms of life, they will be able to sing from their hearts, *The Lord's our Rock, in Him we hide; a Shelter in the time of storm."*

Speaking of hymns, John Q. Adams, sixth president of the United States, and son of John Adams, one of America's most influential *Founding Fathers*, wrote a hymn based on Psalm 43:3, from which the following verse is taken.

"Send forth Thy light and truth and let them lead me still.
Undaunted in the paths of right, up to Thy holy hill.
Then to Thine altar will I spring,
And in my God rejoice and sing."

There was a man...

6

The Preacher, a Place, and a People

Judy Scoggins

There are a few people who come into your life that "NOBODY had better say ANYTHING against!!" Bro. Jimmy Robertson, his lovely wife Frances, and the people of Milldale Baptist Church are such people in my life.

I'll never forget the day I first met Jimmy Robertson. It was in the fall of 1975. I was teaching at a Christian school in Robertsdale, Alabama, and decided to attend a Bible Conference in Pensacola, Florida, to hear a friend, Frank Boydstun, preach. To my surprise, when it was Frank's turn, someone else stepped to the pulpit. My first thought was, *"Who is this? I came to hear Bro. Frank!"* but as soon as that man opened his mouth it was like the house was on fire. I sat there, spellbound. I had never heard anyone preach like he did. After the service I asked Russell Shelton, the pastor and principal of our school, who that was. He said, *"Oh, that was Jimmy Robertson from Milldale."* Well, I had heard about Milldale, and what God was doing there, so I said, *"No wonder he preaches like that!"*

From that point on, every time my fellow teacher and friend, Karen Holland (later, Karen Archer), heard that Bro. Jimmy was preaching within driving distance, we would go to hear him. We were singers, and as it turned out, we ended up singing in several of his meetings. He'd tell about Milldale Baptist Church and the camp meetings and how revival would break out. He shared how people would be found crying out to God in repentance all over the grounds, half the night. He'd talk about victories, trials, and miraculous answers to prayer. He told of the sweet fellowship among the people of the church as

The Milldale Story

they worked on the buildings, in the dining hall and when they worshiped together. He'd say, *"If you want to see a New Testament example of a loving church, follow me to Milldale."* I found myself yearning to be in a place like that.

A new chapter

God saw the desire of our hearts, and in His providence Karen and I ended up spending the next summer at Milldale, helping out in the print shop and serving in the dining room. I remember the atmosphere of the whole place being charged with the presence of God. I had never experienced a body of believers who would meet on Sunday to rehearse what God had been doing in their lives all week long, then with joy on their faces, respond to Him in thanksgiving, praise and worship.

By the end of the summer it felt like Milldale was really my home. Then, to my utter amazement, God allowed this to come to pass within the next year. Milldale's secretary, Rhonda Cutrer (Galipeau), decided to go to college, and Bro. Jimmy asked me to return to Milldale as secretary and church pianist. Ivan Carlson and Danny Greig brought a trailer and loaded up all my earthly possessions to move me to, what I felt, was the Promised Land!

I would soon be reminded again that Milldale Baptist is not a "mega" church, but just a small congregation where an all-powerful God was using a pastor who was willing to lay everything on the altar—who was willing to trust, pray, and obey what God told him to do.

I would also discover that Milldale is not made up of people of great renown or perfect lives, but of regular sinners, saved by God's amazing grace, who put their faith in an Omnipotent God. Together, this dedicated pastor and people have seen God perform miracle after miracle as they've touched the world with the Gospel. It's impossible to overemphasize the impact this church has had on my life for over 35 years. They have been my "family of God."

There was a man...

I've been privileged to know some great men of God, but I've also seen God use common people as prayer warriors such as Ruth Hornsby, Sue Richards, Betty Martin, Lena Partin, and others. He puts each person in the body of Christ with his or her unique gifts. I've witnessed a true "New Testament Church" at Milldale.

After Bro. Jimmy performed my wedding ceremony, my husband, Mel McClellan, took me to where he pastored, about 70 miles away. Then, after working in evangelism for a period of time, God called us to a pastorate in Colorado for the next 18 years. When Mel became ill, the Milldale church sent Gordon McDaniel, Clinton Lee, and Bo Simpson 1,400 miles to move us back to Milldale. The church ministered to us in ways that I can't even explain.

Bro. Jimmy and Frances became my "forever pastor and wife" who were by my side when the Lord called Mel home. For the next three years, I was privileged to be part of the Milldale church again until, in 2005, God sent a wonderful widower, Bill Scoggins, into my life. I returned to Colorado to marry him, but have been able to continue my relationship with my Milldale family by continuing to work with *Fires of Revival*. Bill and I also would not miss any opportunity to participate in the camp meetings and to worship with our friends at the church.

My prayer

As you continue reading *The Milldale Story*, my prayer is that God will rekindle the fire of your own faith.

If you are a pastor, I pray that you will be encouraged to get a word from God about your own ministry, believe that He will perform what He says He will do through you, and follow with unswerving faith to see God use you where He has planted you—whether you are in a large church or a small country church.

The Milldale Story

If you are a layman, I pray that your faith will be increased, and you will have a burning desire for God to use you as you support your pastor, find the areas in which God has gifted you for service, and then get on with taking your place in the body of Christ and witnessing to a lost world.

If you are a woman, I pray that you will see that just as Jesus used many women during His earthly ministry to support and carry on His work, the women of Milldale have been a vital part of its ministry. God can use you in immeasurable ways.

The Milldale Story is not just about a man and a ministry; it is about prayer, faith, revival, and worship. May it challenge your faith to believe what the large letters say across the back wall of the worship tabernacle at Milldale:

"FAITHFUL IS HE THAT CALLETH YOU WHO ALSO WILL DO IT" (I Thess. 5:24)

A testimony—Bill Scoggins[11]

"My first real taste of Milldale came at the February, 2005 Conference where I was exposed to some of the best preaching I had ever heard. It's hard to believe that a small rural Louisiana Church would have such an extensive ministry, but I have learned that anything is possible if you have the faith to believe and the faith to step out on what God has said. I am thankful to our Lord that Jimmy Robertson has had that kind of faith, a faith that has not only enabled him to provide the facilities, but also to bring together some of the greatest ministers of God's Word.

Thank you, Bro. Jimmy, for your ministry and your faithfulness to our Lord. And a special thank you for the part God had you play in bringing Judy into my life!

---

[11] Holiday Island, Arkansas

Section Two

A Tree is Planted

- Ground is just ground until God selects it for His purposes.
- A Midian Desert bush was just a bush until God set it on fire.
- Mt. Sinai was just a mountain until God descended in His glory.
- The Promised Land was just barren ground until, in God's hands, it blossomed like a rose.
- Golgotha was just a hill until its brow was impaled with the cross of the Savior.
- The Upper Room was just a room, until the Holy Spirit descended on the Day of Pentecost.

7

A Church is Born

*"Blessed is the man...whose delight is in the law of the Lord...He is **like a tree** planted by streams of water that yields its fruit every season, and its leaf does not wither. In all that he does, he prospers"* (Psalm 1:1-3).

It is HIS work

The story of God's miraculous intervention in the affairs of man; the testimony of ***His*** mighty works down through history, is really *"HISstory"* fleshed out through ***His*** people who, surrendered to Him, become instruments in ***His*** hands to perform ***His*** purposes in their generation.

There are scores of *ordinary people,* some known to us and some known only to God, who heard "the summons," who followed, and who "accomplished exploits" in their generation in the name and power of the One who called.

And so it was in 1963, that God summoned this son of Tickfaw, Louisiana, **Jimmy Robertson,** who was pastoring Bluff Creek Baptist Church in East Feliciana Parish, to take a step of faith and purchase a piece of land near Zachary.[12]

Where's that?

Zachary? *"Where's that?"* asked Ron Dunn, the first time he was invited to speak at Milldale. He would soon learn that finding the town of Zachary was going to be a lot easier than finding the Milldale Camp Meeting grounds. He got lost, not

---

[12] Zachary, named for Darel Zachary, the unfortunate farmer who, in the mid 1800's, reacting to the Illinois Central Railroad's plans to lay track through his property, sold George Brown the 160 acres where the city would be incorporated in 1889. The price? $100. He left the area, never to return.

only that first time, but every subsequent year he preached at Milldale. He was not alone. Many others lost their bearings on at least their first try.

But these sixteen acres were more than just a piece of land to Jimmy Robertson. This part of Louisiana had a history—a history of mighty movings of God. It was a place where, in years past, God had been pleased to visit. It was to this area that thousands of people came year after year from all over the country to hear the passionate "revival preaching" of those early Methodists, such as Billy Sunday, who were on fire for God.

As has already been mentioned, Jimmy shared the vision God had given him with his dear friends, Sonny Holland, Jesse Norris, and Manley Beasley, a vision of providing a place where, once again, those "thirsting in spirit" could come and drink of God's living water.

Laying the Foundation

"For no other foundation can anyone lay than that which is laid, which is Christ Jesus" (1 Corinthians 3:11).

There were no bands playing, no TV cameras or radio microphones, no big-name guests to attract a crowd that August 4, Sunday morning, in 1963. There were just 15 people and a young man who had left his pastorate at Bluff Creek Baptist Church in Clinton, Louisiana, to start a church, out in the country, 15 miles north of Baton Rouge. He had come with no promise of salary; there were no buildings; all he had was a piece of paper on which was written the purchase agreement he had made with the land owner.

But Jimmy Robertson had arrived with more than a dream of buying land and planting a church. He had come with a vision to see a supernatural God do a supernatural work. He had come with a burden for those who were perishing without Christ. He had come with a broken heart over prayerless, backsliding churches all across America who needed to hear the message of faith, prayer and revival. He came, holding on to 1 Thessalonians 5:24, *"Faithful is he that calleth you, who also will do it."*

Bro. Jimmy faced those 15 people who had joined him for that first service on that hot, humid, August morning, with a commitment to make the preaching of God's Word and the exalting of the Lord Jesus Christ the cornerstone of this new congregation. He had observed fads come and go, and he knew that the only thing that would abide forever was the Word of God. He had seen personalities rise and fall, and he had observed an abundance of man's wisdom being preached from the pulpits of the land. He knew that that was not for him, but chose rather to be like the person described in Psalm 1:1-3 (NKJV).

Blessed is the man who walks not in the counsel of the ungodly,
Nor stands in the path of sinners,
Nor sits in the seat of the scornful;
But his delight is in the law of the Lord,
And in His law he meditates day and night.
<u>He shall be like a tree planted by the rivers of water</u>,
That brings forth its fruit in its season,
Whose leaf also shall not wither;
And whatsoever he does shall prosper.

A testimony—Muriel Norris

"My husband, Jesse Norris, had been invited to preach a meeting at Bluff Creek Baptist Church in Clinton, Louisiana. He had been there before, but this time he wanted the family to accompany him. He had already met the pastor, Jimmy Robertson, when he was in revival at Gardner, in the Alexandria area, and I remember Jesse describing that young eighteen year old as a dynamic, choice servant, and one God was going to use greatly in His church. Now, a few years later, Bro. Jimmy was the pastor of Bluff Creek Baptist Church, was married to a beautiful young lady, and they had already started their family.

"While in this meeting at the Bluff Creek church, Bro. Jimmy shared a vision with us that God had given him. It was a vision for a Camp Meeting ministry. They prayed together, and it was not long before my husband felt God would have us move from the Pineville, Louisiana area, where we had been living, to join this young pastor in this new ministry endeavor near Zachary, Louisiana. So, on a June morning in 1964, we began our journey south.

"From the beginning, the meetings at Milldale were unforgettable. God's *Amazing Grace* was evident as we experienced the flow of God's Spirit, almost like a tsunami, covering the entire congregation. It didn't matter if it was a large conference, our local church with its faithful few, or just two or three gathered in the prayer chapel, you were aware of God's presence, and once you've experienced that, you'll never forget it, and you'll never be satisfied with anything less."

A Word from Bro. Jimmy

The reason there is so little repentance in most churches today is that there is little preaching of the unadulterated Word of God. Jeremiah 23:29 tells us that the Word of God is like a **crushing hammer**. Through the prophet God proclaims, *"Is not my word...like a hammer that breaketh the rock in pieces?"* It can break the hardest hearts.

Ezekiel 37:7 says that it is a **life-giving force.** The prophet said, *"So I prophesied as I was commanded: and as I prophesied, there was a noise, and behold a shaking, and the bones came together, bone to his bone."* Think of it. God spoke life into dead bones.

The Milldale Story

Ephesians 6:17 says that it is a **weapon of defense.** This passage admonishes us to *"take the helmet of salvation, and the sword of the Spirit, which is the word of God."*

Hebrews 4:12 describes it further as a **probing instrument.** *"For the word of God is quick and powerful, and sharper than any two-edged sword, piercing even to the dividing asunder of soul and spirit, and of the joints and marrow, and is a discerner of the thoughts and intents of the heart."* That ought to shake us and cause us to pay attention to the awesome Word of God!

Then turning to Psalm 119:9, we read where God's word is described as a **purifier of life.** *"Wherewithal shall a young man cleanse his way? By taking heed thereto according to thy word."*

And in John 15:3, Jesus says: *"Now ye are clean through the word which I have spoken unto you."* Again in John 17:17, Jesus refers to the **cleansing work of the Word.** He prays: *"Sanctify them through thy truth; thy word is truth."*

In Ephesians 5:26 we read that Christ loved the church and gave Himself for her. *"That he might sanctify and cleanse it* (the church) *with the washing of water by the word."*

Finally, in Romans 1:16, the Apostle Paul reminds us that the Word is the **power of God unto salvation.** No wonder he wrote to the Corinthian church that he had not come *"preaching enticing words of man's wisdom, but in the demonstration and power of the Holy Ghost"* (1 Corinthians 2:4).

That's what I wanted to see more than anything else when I came to Milldale. I had decided never to settle for less than preaching in the demonstration and power of the Holy Ghost and not in the enticing words of man's wisdom. I knew that if it was going to happen, God was going to have to do it, and through the years that is what He has done, without fail.

It was at Milldale—Mike Courtney[13]

"I was exposed to the Milldale ministry in 1973, soon after the Lord Jesus Christ saved me by His grace and called me into the ministry.

"*It was at Milldale,* early in my Christian life, that I learned what it meant to live by faith, to have a consistent prayer life, to stay in the Word of God. *It was at Milldale* I learned that the Spirit-filled life is a legitimate experience for the child of God, without the excesses you see in some places. *It was at Milldale* in those early days, that the Lord placed a burden and desire in my heart for real, biblical revival, both individually and corporately. As I told someone, *"I was born in the fire and can't stand only smoke!" It was at Milldale* that I learned about Spirit-filled giving that goes beyond the tithe. *It was at Milldale* that I learned that the consequence of real revival is missions and evangelism.

"I guess you could say that just about everything I know, everything I believe, and everything I am today in my life and ministry, the Lord taught me and made me through Milldale. So, needless to say, I praise God for Milldale Baptist Church, and especially for Jimmy Robertson and Danny Greig. *"To God be the glory, great things He has done,"* and continues to do in and through Milldale!"

---

[13] Mike Courtney, evangelist, Garland, Texas

8

A Branch Begins to Grow
The Camp Meeting

Camp Meetings were a phenomenon of American frontier Christianity that filled a religious vacuum all across the land. The Cane Ridge, Kentucky, Camp Meeting in 1801, when Baptists, Methodists and Presbyterians gathered by the thousands, is considered to be the most important one in American history. The Cane Ridge Camp Meeting played an important spiritual role during what is called, "The Second Great Awakening."

"The tent[14] was filled beyond capacity. It was rated to seat around four hundred, but that night there must have been nearly five hundred crammed inside, with another hundred gathered around the outside," recalls Jimmy Robertson. "We were all set to begin our first Milldale Camp Meeting on that Monday, August 3, 1964, exactly one year, less a day, since we had held our first church service."

And what a year it had been. A month after Bro. Jimmy had challenged that group of fifteen to begin believing God for the impossible, he began to advertise what that little church on Milldale Road was planning to do. A brochure was soon sent to every evangelical church in the state of Louisiana, announcing:

"We're going to have a camp meeting beginning the first Monday in August. Everyone welcome. Meals and lodging free."

---

[14] This was the tent Jimmy Robertson purchased for his evangelistic crusades in the early days of his ministry.

God had made it clear that they were not to charge for anything. They were going to trust God to provide. To the uninitiated observer, however, this would have been hard to believe. Meals? OK. But lodging? The only building on the 16 Milldale acres was a little house the church was meeting in, and it could only seat 25-30 people. Where were they going to house those who would come expecting to find a bed to sleep on?

Jimmy Robertson looks back

As a church, we began to pray. We began to trust God, and we began to work. Huey Collier almost single-handedly cleared the grounds. All the men and women of the church pitched in joyously. The first thing we were able to do was build the little red brick church which gave us a preaching area that would also serve as a dining hall. We then turned one of the small side rooms into a kitchen. Now that we had the meal service taken care of, the next step of faith was building a place to lodge the folk. We had no funds; we had no friends; all we had was God, and that's the best place to be.

I'll never forget the day we started to talk about building the first dormitory. My brother, Ray,[15] said to me, *"I have some timber. We can cut that up into lumber."* I said, *"We don't have time for it to dry."* Ray said: *"We'll take it to the mill and trade it for lumber."* So, Bro. Jesse Norris, Ray and some others went and cut down the timber, took it to the sawmill and traded it for lumber to build our first dormitory.

Time and again we found ourselves at road's end without any money to buy materials for the next week, but by the time we needed it, we had it. God sent us Bob Holland, Bro. Sonny's brother, who was a building contractor. He not only worked

---

[15] Jimmy's whole family, beginning with his father, Ray O. Robertson, were very instrumental in not only helping the ministry get started, but by standing with him, "holding the ropes," through the years.

with us on this first dormitory but oversaw the construction of several other buildings during those early years. We proved over and over again that *God abideth faithful*, and by the time Monday, August 3, rolled around, He had supplied every need we had!

And here they came—all one hundred fifty who had made lodging reservations. We put them in the dormitory; we put them in homes, and we put some in Sunday School rooms. Then in addition to those who were staying on the grounds, hundreds arrived from the surrounding area. The parking lot was full and cars were parked all up and down the highway. The tent was packed. Everything was ready.

The storm

I knew a storm was approaching. I could hear the thunder in the distance, and the tent flaps began to wave in the wind. I could tell it was going to be a big one. I called Bro. Jesse Norris, Manley Beasley, and Sonny Holland to step outside with me. I said, *"Don't you think we ought to dismiss this crowd?"* I'd no sooner gotten those words out of my mouth than one of Job's comforters ran up: *"The radio is warning that this storm is going to be a real bad one. We should get everybody out of here as soon as possible because we're not going to be able to have a service in this weather. They say it could be dangerous."*

"I looked at Manley Beasley, and I'll never forget what he said. Now you'd have to know him to appreciate this.

"Bro. Jimmy, we're not going to send the folk home. We're going to ask God to turn the storm around. Bro. Jimmy, we're going to have a meeting."

We went to prayer, and as we did I could hear, and even see the rain approaching in the distance. We prayed, and as we finished praying the storm began to shift. We watched it approach us from the left; then we watched it turn and circle around us to the right. It went all the way around the tent. We stood there witnessing the hand of God cause a storm to do His bidding. Not a drop of rain fell on that tent! Not a drop of rain! Everyone was protected from the storm."

God, the Weather-Maker

Weather has played a significant role in God's economy throughout history. Scripture is full of accounts when He used the elements to either display His awesomeness, teach His children a lesson, or punish evil. He used it to punish the rebelliousness of mankind when He sent the first rainfall and flooded the entire earth. He used it for a teaching point on the Sea of Galilee when Peter was taught a lesson about keeping his eyes on the Master. He used the elements to demonstrate His awesome power at the climax of the crucifixion when all the fury of His judgment of sin descended on His Son as darkness covered the land for three hours, and an earthquake split the rocks and opened graves.

God used a storm on a lonely English meadow, one day, where a pastor, Augustus Toplady, was walking. Being acquainted with the area, he quickly ran to a crevice in a large nearby rock in which he took shelter, as the lightening flashed, the thunder rolled and the rain descended in torrents. As the storm raged, Pastor Toplady's mind turned to Isaiah 26: 4 that, in the King James margin reads, *"Trust ye in the Lord forever, for in the Lord Jehovah is the Rock of Ages."* As he mused on that verse, the first lines of the familiar hymn began to etch themselves in his heart:

Rock of Ages, cleft for me, let me hide myself in Thee.
Let the water and the blood,
From Thy wounded side which flowed,
Be of sin the double cure, save from wrath and make me pure.

The Milldale Story

Upon returning home, he wrote the remaining verses, words that have so profoundly impacted millions over the years, a reminder of the solid foundation on which we stand.

God used a violent storm to catch the attention of John Newton and draw him out of his drunkenness and slave trading to become one of his generation's most beloved pastors and hymn writers. Who has not been touched by his *Amazing Grace,* the most popular hymn in history?

And God decided to provide an extra boost to the inauguration of the *Milldale Camp Meeting* ministry by redirecting a storm that everyone knew could have carried that gospel tent into the next parish, and could have caused injury to many inside. The storm, instead, provided free publicity. The enemy was wanting to use the elements to shut everything down, but God intended to use the weather for His glory. And He did!

Bro. Jimmy recalls how the word got out, and people began coming from Baton Rouge and the surrounding area, asking, *"Is this the place where God turned the storm around?"* It was!

"They had heard what God had done on our behalf and they wanted to be where He was," continues Jimmy. "And folks, did we ever have a Camp Meeting. I'll tell you, the glory of God came down. The power of God settled on that place. We preached, we prayed, we sang, and heaven came down. God touched and stirred the hearts of the people. We had a Holy Ghost, old-fashioned revival meeting like most folk never see in a lifetime. God was faithful. God was faithful to His Word."

This emphasis on God's Word is the reason some of the greatest Bible expositors of our generation have preached at Milldale Camp Meetings. They came to proclaim God's Word. In those early days, in addition to the guest speakers, you would hear the powerful preaching of regulars, Bro. Jesse Norris, Manley Beasley, Sonny Holland, Ron Dunn, J. Harold Smith, Curtis McCarley and others.

A Tree is Planted

Standing behind the pulpit on any given night, preaching with their heavy Scottish accents, might be James Alexander Stewart, so mightily used of God in eastern and western Europe, or Duncan Campbell, who was God's instrument in the Hebrides Revival in the 1940's. Added to the Scottish brogue were the British accents of Roy Hession and Major Ian Thomas.

At other times you might see a man in a white suit making his way to the podium. R. G. Lee, pastor of Bellevue Baptist Church, had driven down from Memphis to be a part of the Milldale ministry. Or, it could be Dr. Oswald J. Smith, one of the world's most influential missionary statesmen, who founded and pastored the famous People's Church in Toronto.

"Very few escaped the deep conviction of the Holy Spirit when Leonard Ravenhill, who lived for several years at Milldale, called God's people to return to Him," recalls Bro. Jimmy. "And Hyman Appelman, who was often with us, never failed to bring us to our knees. Then there were Dr. C. L. Culpepper and Miss Bertha Smith, bringing us first hand reports of the mighty moving of the Holy Spirit in the Shantung Revival in China."

The list of speakers[16] who have stood behind the Milldale Camp-Meeting pulpit could be likened to a "who's who" of evangelical, revival-oriented leaders, and they, under God's guidance, were used over the years to keep the focus where it needed to be. This has been the uniqueness of Milldale's Camp Meeting ministry—this ever-growing branch of the Milldale tree.

A testimony—Malcom Ellis[17]

"The Labor Day Conference in 1988, marked the beginning of my lifelong love for, and affiliation with this place called Milldale. I have attended at least one Conference a year since

---

[16] See page 254 for list of Milldale Camp Meeting Preachers
[17] Malcom Ellis, evangelist, Colmeseil, Texas

then, and many years have attended every scheduled meeting. How can I describe what God has done in me through the preaching of Ron Dunn, Manley Beasley, Bro. Jesse Norris, Ed Greig, along with the multitudes of others who were part of the preaching program at Milldale during those early years? I felt like a kid in knee britches around those men of God. I was literally in awe of them. But I soon learned that they were not the awesome ones—it was their God who was to be held in awe, and they were simply men of faith who dared to trust God and attempt great things in His great name.

"Since those early days the men and women of God who make up the Milldale family have become some of the dearest people on earth to me and mine. I am so thankful for the sovereign arrangement of God that allowed me to meet Bro. Jimmy and Bro. Sonny when I was just a kid preacher. Since then, Bro. Danny Greig has become one of my dearest friends—a man of God in whom I have unbounded confidence, and for whom I have the deepest respect.

The local church
"I've had opportunity to preach several revival meetings in the Milldale Baptist Church through the years, allowing me to know the membership of this local church in ways that I would have never come to know them as merely a Conference participant. They are a people who have given selflessly and labored tirelessly through the years to minister to hurting and hungry people from across America and around the world.

The family
"In conclusion, I want to say a word as a husband and father. I am most grateful to the Lord Jesus for providing a place like Milldale where I can bring my wife and son to find refreshment in Christ in this dry and barren land of religious harlotry. Milldale is for us a *haven of rest,* a cool shady spot to sit for a while and just hear Jesus speak. In the nation and

generation in which we are living, like-minded Christians are few and far between. It is difficult to find "believers" who see any need for revival and radical repentance in the church. Most seem to be perfectly content with a business-as-usual church life, and the motions of a dead religion.

"Milldale is, for my family, an oasis in *'a dry and thirsty land where no water is.'* I thank God that my son has been able to grow up in the company of some of the greatest men of God the world has ever known—to hear them preach regularly, to know them by name, and to see how God can use people who are wholly given up to Him.

"Thank you Bro. Jimmy, Sonny, Danny, and the multitudes of other men and women of Milldale who have given of yourselves over the years to build and maintain the Milldale Bible Conference. I am a life that has been affected for eternity by what you have given unto the Lord. My family has benefited in more ways than words can tell because of your sacrifices."

9

The Camp Meeting Branch
keeps growing

Year two

A testimony—Herb Reavis, Jr. [18]

"As a recent addition to the Milldale family, I believe that its conference ministry is needed now more than ever. The hour is desperate; Christ is coming, and the church is slipping into apostasy.

"Milldale is the only place, that I know of, that continues to preach the themes of *the Christ life, the faith life, the giving life and the witnessing life* all in one conference. At Milldale, the focus is not on a breakout session but on the breaking out of the Holy Spirit in REVIVAL. To be a part of this ministry is one of the highlights of my life."

Before the first Camp had ended, plans were in the making for the next year's ministry—there would be two Camp Meetings. Knowing that they were going to need additional facilities, Bro. Jimmy and his small band of believers began building, battling and believing.

Bro. Jimmy recalls:

"We decided to set up two-shift days—eight hours each, sixteen hours a day. I was preaching many revival meetings

---

[18] Dr. Reavis is the senior pastor of North Jacksonville Baptist Church, Jacksonville, Florida.

back then, and during one of those periods I preached six weeks in a row. But that didn't keep me from helping with the work. Many times I would drive home from a revival late Friday night, get up Saturday morning, cook breakfast for the crew at 6 o'clock, then help them work until I left early afternoon for the next revival meeting. Before I left, I'd have the next crew all lined up. People came, people worked, people gave, people sacrificed, people prayed, and the amazing thing about it all was the joy everyone was experiencing in joining God in fulfilling the vision He had given.

"People never thought about what it was costing them. Everyone was looking at what was being gained, and the gain was not just seeing dormitories "A," "B" and "C" finished, it was seeing another tool made available for God to use for His glory. Buildings are just wood, brick or mortar, like everything else that is temporal, until God uses them for the advancement of His Kingdom."

Year three

By now building "D" had been finished and "C" was being used as a dining hall. The Milldale facilities could now sleep around 700 for each camp meeting. Then, added to these were the "off campus" attendees.

And the people came. They came from across America—singles, couples, families—February, June, July, August and Thanksgiving weekends. Not only were the dorms filled to capacity, but trailers and campers dotted the campgrounds, and scores were put up in the homes of church members—everybody doing his and her part. Each building, each piece of furniture, each meal, represented sacrificial love on the part of God's children, either through financial giving or hands-on labor, not unlike the building of the Temple we read about in 2 Chronicles 2-4, though perhaps a bit less elaborate!

The Milldale Story

The Tabernacle miracle

It would not be long before Bro. Jimmy sensed that God was about to require them to take another major step of faith—they were going to have to build a meeting hall, a tabernacle that could accommodate the growing crowds. Though they had no money, he was persuaded that *Jehovah Jireh* would be their Provider, and that He was already preparing the way.

Jimmy Robertson remembers

"I had driven by a large abandoned building on Florida Boulevard in Baton Rouge for several years, and each time I passed it, I thought, *'That building sure would make a good tabernacle.'* I finally decided to check on who owned it and learned that it belonged to an attorney. I contacted him, and we worked out a deal that, if we would take the building down and clear up the lot, he would let us have the structure. That was the beginning of an adventure in which we saw the miraculous hand of God at work.

"I announced to the church what we were planning to do, and along with a group of our men, including Bro. Manley, Sonny Holland and Jesse Norris, we headed for Florida Boulevard. The first thing on the agenda was removing the metal roof, and that proved to be no small chore. Some days the only ones working on the site were Manley, Sonny, Jesse and me. We had a time.

"After the roof was removed the next thing we had to do was take down the heavy steel trusses. The "experts" told us that we would not be able to take them down in one piece by ourselves because some of them were 120 feet long. They said that we would have to hire an engineer to get it done, but when they told us what it was going to cost, I told them that we didn't have that kind of money, and that we would do it ourselves. And we did.

"I hired a crane, and we watched as the operator attached the top of those trusses to the crane neck; and as he began lowering them down it looked like the trusses were bending double, but when they were placed on the ground, they straightened out without a kink in them! We then took them apart so we could haul them off to Milldale where we began to build the tabernacle with our own hands.

"When we finally got the steel set up and were ready to pour the cement, I said: *'Well folk, I didn't tell you that we don't have a dollar for the cement. We've done everything we've known to do and now we're going to have to trust God for the money to go on from here.'*

"We prayed and asked God to send what we needed.

Jehovah Jireh
"My wife, Frances, had prepared lunch for the crew, so we headed for the house to eat. As we sat down around the table the phone rang. It was Tom Hudson, an oilman from Oklahoma.

'Bro. Jimmy, do you need any money at Milldale? I have $10,000 that I need to give away, so I thought I'd call you to ask who I should give it to.'
'Well,' I said, *'if you hadn't asked me who you should give it to I would have been delighted to take it, but, Scripture says, 'Let every man look on the needs of his brother,' and Harold Brown at the Fairhaven Children's Home, needs money for a building as much as we do, so I'm going to tell you to send the money to him.'* Bro. Tom got real quiet. Finally he said:
'Well, I'm gonna play a game with you. I had no idea that you were going to tell me to give the money to someone else, so what I'm going to do is send $10,000 to Milldale and $10,000 to the Fairhaven Children's Home.'

"A check arrived in the mail a couple days later. We poured the cement and continued to see miracle after miracle as the tabernacle went up.

The Milldale Story

"T.C. Hudson, and his sons Philip and Zack, were a blessing to Milldale over the years as they continued to send timely gifts. Milldale is indebted to the Hudson family for being used of the Lord to stand with us in this way. Philip, the preacher son, also has blessed us by speaking at the Milldale camp meetings over the years."

A testimony—Jerry Spencer [19]

"To some, the term *Camp Meeting* conjures up visions of excess emotionalism. This can never be said of the camp meetings at Milldale. Over the past four decades I've attended around 100 meetings, including the Youth Camps, and I've never observed any shallow fleshly behavior. I've seen lots of exuberance, enthusiasm, excitement and rejoicing, but never have I witnessed anything that was unsavory or out of bounds.

"Milldale's purpose has always been to glorify God and honor the Lord Jesus Christ. An integral part of this goal, is the exultation of the Word of God. Sound doctrine is the order of the day, and those who stand behind the Milldale pulpit are expected to preach sound biblical messages. The message you'll hear at Milldale is a balanced biblical truth that promotes the principles of Scripture.

"Milldale has intentionally steered clear of cultish hobby horses. They have refused to get on the bandwagon of theological fads or fringe issues. Evangelism, missions, revival, and Spirit-filled living have always been its emphasis. Those attending Milldale Camp Meetings sense the liberty of the Holy Spirit that results in a freedom to worship, while those who may lean toward more shallow exhibitions of the flesh will probably find themselves out of place. The very atmosphere discourages abnormal and unbiblical behavior.

"The meetings at Milldale go beyond the joyous blessings of corporate worship, however. There has always been an

---

[19] Pastor and evangelist, Dothan, Alabama

emphasis upon repentance, personal holiness and daily Spirit-filled living. This results in changed lives as people return to their homes and churches better Christians, better fathers, mothers, husbands, wives, better church members and witnesses for Christ. Pastors return revived, more passionate and more deeply committed to serving the Lord Jesus and being all that God has called them to be."

A testimony—Jimmy Autin[20]

"I believe what God has done through Milldale Baptist Church has helped me become the man God has called me to be today. I once was a boy with no hope, lost and confused. God saved me in 1986, and now I am a husband, a dad, and a pastor! Many of my friends have also been changed through the ministry of Milldale."

---

[20] Pastor, Bethel Baptist Church, Grand Bois, Louisiana

10

Teen Camps

Another Branch

A testimony—Jerry Spencer[21]

"I have often wondered how many hundreds of young people were saved during the two decades I served as camp pastor at the Milldale Youth Camps. I also wonder where many are today. It is my opinion that hundreds are faithful members of local churches. Some are deacons, Sunday School teachers and women's ministry leaders. There are pastors, evangelists and missionaries out there who are faithfully proclaiming the gospel. Many have married, established good Christian homes, and have raised their children in the nurture and admonition of the Lord. And it is so exciting for me to see many of them bringing their children and grandchildren back to the Milldale Teen Camps."

The underlying purpose in establishing the Teen Camp branch of the Milldale tree is well summarized in the following Psalms.

"Wherewithal shall a young man cleanse his way? By taking heed thereto according to thy word. With my whole heart have I sought thee: O let me not wander from thy commandments. Thy word have I hid in mine heart that I might not sin against thee" (Psalm 119:9-11).

---

[21] Pastor/evangelist, Dothan, Alabama

A Tree is Planted

To introduce young people to the claims of Christ while teaching them how to hide God's Word in their hearts so that, as they grow older they'll not stray from its teachings, was and is the goal of Milldale's Teen Camp ministry.

This does not mean that there are no fun and games at Milldale. *"Au contrair,"* as Louisiana Cajuns would say. Looking for sports? Take your pick—basketball, volleyball, softball, soccer, swimming (not co-ed), you name it. Add to these the impromptu competitions that add color to the day, such as…boxing?

Boxing? Not a bit over-the-top for a Christian camp? Jerry Spencer recalls a memorable moment that took place one year during his stint as Camp Pastor.

The fight

"One of my most entertaining memories during those years had to do with two sons of the famous evangelist, Manley Beasley. Manley Jr., nicknamed Bubba, and his younger brother Steve, who, like his father, was dyslexic and was going through an especially frustrating period, got into a scuffle.

"Steve had kept bugging his big brother until, on this particular day, Bubba, who really didn't want to fight with his younger brother, had to defend himself. This soon resulted in the beginning of a good round of fisticuffs which in turn attracted a crowd.

"The camp recreation director came running, pulled them apart, and realizing that there were still some pent-up emotions, he decided to let them resume their fight, but in a less dangerous fashion. *'If you're gonna fight let's do it right.'*

"He got two pairs of oversized boxing gloves, put them on the boys and said: *'Now, have at it!'* They lunged at each other, flailing the air while doing little damage because of the huge gloves. Soon they were not able to hold their arms up any longer and they fell to the ground, laughing up a storm."

The Milldale Story

"Boys will be boys, and boys grow up to be men, and both of these sons of Manley Beasley, as well as his other two children, Jonathan and Debbie, have gone on to serve their Lord, as have countless other young people whose lives were impacted by the ministry of Milldale's youth camps."

Afterglow

It was, and is, a wonderful sight to see young people shedding tears of repentance, then tears of joy as they are transferred from the kingdom of darkness into the kingdom of light. On the last night, the leaders would have all the young people who had been saved line up across the front. It was not unusual to see 100 or more converts professing faith in Christ.

After the evening worship services, youth groups from various churches would then meet together in secluded areas for what is called *Afterglow*. This was a time of sharing with each other, talking with their counselors, and getting their questions answered. These were amazing times when many advanced from being a religious church member into being an authentic born-again Christian. Interestingly, over the years, even some counselors have been converted, including pastors and wives.

These small-group afterglow meetings continue to be a vital part of the youth camp ministry, and today, it is exciting to see how many of these sessions are now being led by counselors who met the Lord at Milldale years ago.

And of course, as has been true since Adam saw Eve, boys still notice girls, and girls still notice boys. More than a few have met their future life-partner at Milldale.

Last day

The last day of camp is talent and skit day. It's always a lot of fun to watch the young people display amazing creativity. Then, after the evening meal, the week closes with a worship service that climaxes in a *call to the called*—a call to full time ministry.

A most rewarding moment for camp leaders is when they see young people lined up all across the front of the worship center. Sometimes it would take an hour or more as each one shared what God was calling him or her to do. Many true champions announced their call during those services, including:

Jason Robertson, son of Bro. Jimmy's brother, Ed, who went on to graduate from Liberty University and New Orleans Baptist Seminary and who now pastors a church he started in California.

Philip Robertson, son of Jimmy's brother, Louis, who graduated from Liberty University and New Orleans Seminary and now pastors in Louisiana. Philip has served as President of the Louisiana Baptist Convention.

Dan Spencer, announced his call at Milldale and now pastors in Georgia and is currently serving as President of the Georgia Baptist Convention.

These are but three of the hundreds who, having answered God's call at Milldale, are serving the Lord around the world."

A testimony—Bill Britt[22]

"Part of the vision that Bro. Jimmy had for Milldale was to touch the hearts of teenagers across the country. For eleven years I had the honor of being camp evangelist at the Pre-teen and Teen Retreats. It has been exciting to see hundreds of students travel from all over the country to attend these camps, and there is an untold number of young men and women who have been saved through this ministry. But not only have many been saved, there are scores of men and women all around the globe serving the Lord Jesus who were called to the Gospel ministry through the Milldale camps. It was not uncommon to see a dozen or more teenagers surrender to the Lord's call in a single service.

---

[22] Evangelist, Gallatin, Tennessee. Also see testimony on page 244.

The Milldale Story

"On more than one occasion the evening services would be extended longer than the planned time in order to allow the Holy Spirit to move in our hearts. These times would spill over into the group share times that would later on break out into revival in the different churches represented.

"Now that I have been part of the camps at Milldale for all these years, I have people come to me in churches across the country to testify of how their lives were changed at Milldale. Some of those who attended as a teenager are now sending their own teenagers to Milldale. But, it is not only the students who have been blessed—many of the counselors who came with the students have been saved, revived, or called to the ministry. I have received reports through the years from adults who had come with their students, about how the Lord changed their lives.

"Milldale is basically a Bible camp. There are numerous opportunities for the students to be taught the Word each day during the course of the week. But, there is also adequate time for fun and recreation. One of my joys each summer was to take on the challenge of seeing how many young men it would take to "dunk" me in the swimming pool. And might I say that the number has yet to be discovered! "Big Poppa," as the students affectionately called me, enjoyed just hangin' and chillin' with students and hearing their dreams for their lives as well as their heartaches and disappointments.

"One particular group of students had been attending another camp for many years. Upon the announcement from the student pastor that they would not be going to that particular camp, but instead to Milldale, the students voiced their disappointment because the camp they had been attending was much larger and had more "bells and whistles" than Milldale. It was exciting and amusing to see the reaction of these groups after they had the "Milldale experience" for a few days. Not only were many of these students' lives transformed, but they registered for the next year and have continued to do so."

11

A Scotsman Arrives

James Alexander Stewart: A common name in Scotland, but his was no common birth, because, *"When the Creator recorded the name of James Alexander, son of John and Agnes Stewart, in the book of heaven before the foundation of the world, it was with a plan and purpose which He had for no other man."*[23]

In James Stewart's relatively brief lifetime, he impacted almost every country in Eastern, Central and Western Europe, through his preaching and writing, and his influence was felt in America and as far away as the Orient. If there was a secret to his life and accomplishments, it was that he was *filled with the Spirit of God* to whom he bowed and with whom he enjoyed constant communion. He was willing to pay the price of total surrender.

The famous Ulster (Northern Ireland) Revivalist, W. P. Nicholson, said of Dr. Stewart, *"Through European countries he has brought thousands to Christ through his teaching and preaching. I have followed him for many years and he has been used of God in mighty revivals in many places. He knows from a long and wide and successful experience what revival is. Many can, and do, write fluently about revivals, but they write about something they have never experienced as fact. James Stewart is different."*

Of all the ways he could be addressed, there were two he preferred most: *James Stewart, Missionary,* or, *James Stewart, Preacher of the Gospel.* Some have called him the 20th century Apostle Paul, for everywhere he went, not only was there a

---

[23] From *James Stewart, Missionary,* by Ruth Stewart. Published by Revival Literature, Asheville, NC. Available at www.revivallit.org

The Milldale Story

large ingathering of souls, but the Body of Christ was built up and churches were planted.

Though his primary focus for much of his ministry was Eastern Europe and the "Lands of Russia," he was used of God in a powerful way wherever he went, as is seen in the following report from Trondheim, Norway.

"The Cathedral was crowded to the doors; people sitting and standing everywhere. The power of God fell on us. It was overwhelming. In this town of 50,000 (now 150,000 where Norway's University of Science and Technology is located) *we had 10,000 men in an open-air meeting in a football park. I spoke 55 times in 10 days. Anxious souls everywhere. I spoke on government radio and they paid me! The newspapers are reporting that even the street cars are moving slowly through Market Square so as not to disturb the stillness of God. A five-minute silence for prayer is called for daily in the center of the city. The Lord is adding daily such as are being saved. Hallelujah!"*[24]

From Scotland to Milldale!

"I had only heard about James Alexander Stewart but had never met him," recalls Bro. Jimmy. "I felt led, however, in November, 1965, to invite him to speak at our next Camp Meeting. I knew it was going to take a miracle because I was sure he had never heard about Milldale and probably had never been to Louisiana. But God is a God of miracles, and what I didn't know at the time was that He was setting in motion a relationship that would eventually impact millions of people around the world."

"It was some time later that I learned from Dr. Stewart's dear wife, Ruth, just how much of a miracle it had been that they had come. I learned again that when God is in something,

---

[24] *James Stewart, Missionary,* Revival Literature, Asheville, NC.

A Tree is Planted

He sure is capable of working out the details. Here is what she told me.

"About a month before your letter reached us, my husband told me that the Holy Spirit had spoken to him that he was going to receive a letter from a man in Louisiana he had never met, to invite him to go to a place he had never heard of, and that God was going to do a supernatural work in that place like they had never seen before, and that it was going to touch the nation. He said, 'I'm going to receive that invitation before we get home.' We were overseas at the time."

Two weeks later a package containing their mail caught up with them, and as Dr. Stewart flipped through the envelopes, he came to the letter of invitation Jimmy Robertson had sent. *"This is the letter I told you I would get,"* he said to his wife, as he opened it. He immediately responded to Bro. Jimmy's invitation: *"We are scheduled to arrive home from Scotland on the Friday before your meeting starts on Monday. We won't even unpack. We'll head right on down to Milldale."*

"I met Dr. Stewart for the first time in the dining hall, which was the tabernacle at that time," recalls Bro. Jimmy. "I'll never forget when he walked in. He was much shorter than I thought he would be. He was just a little man. We shook hands, then he walked to the platform to test the microphone and started to speak in Russian. I thought, *'I hope he knows we speak English here.'*

"That night, James Alexander Stewart preached on revival, and the power of God fell. Not only was the altar filled, but all over the property, behind every tree, people were on their faces before God. You could walk across the grounds and hear folk sobbing in repentance and crying out to God. At three in the morning the altars were still filled. This was not a time when people would come down, kneel for a moment, then go back to their seats. This was a time of doing business with their Maker.

The Milldale Story

We had been praying for Revival, and we were now beginning to see the answer to our prayers.

"Friends, people are not interested in what we can do, they are interested in what God can do. This was in February, 1966, and word began to spread how God had 'showed up.' So many people were now wanting to come that we planned a second, a third, a fourth and a fifth Camp Meeting that year. We were receiving reservations from all over America. People were hungering and thirsting after God.

"And oh, what glory! Every meeting was an encounter with the *Reviver of Hearts*. How I long to see it happen again, and you know, God is the same God. He's still the Faithful One who wants to meet with His people. He is still saying today:

"If my people which are called by my name shall humble themselves, and pray, and seek my face, and turn from their wicked ways, then will I hear from heaven, and will forgive their sins and will heal their land" (2 Chronicles 7:14).

Note: Dr. Stewart had a special affinity for children and young people. At the drop of a hat he would be out playing games with them, and especially football (soccer) as he had been an outstanding player in his early days. This relationship with young people carried over into spiritual matters, such as on his third year of ministering at Milldale.

He had arrived several days early in order to be a part of the prayer times that were always scheduled prior to every camp meeting. On one of these occasions he was asked to speak on the subject of prayer, and because school was out, there were a number of youth in attendance. As he looked at those gathered he felt led to address the young people specifically.

Dr. Stewart: "Many of you will soon be graduating from high school, and some of you will be going on to college where you are going to face people who will be skeptical of what you believe. They are going to try to get you to doubt your salvation and even question the very existence of God. The best way for you to get a foundation that will stand against the enemy is for you to see God work. So, instead of my speaking on prayer this morning, we're going to ask God to answer a specific prayer request in a way that we'll know He has heard and answered." Turning to Jimmy Robertson, he asked:

"Why isn't the Prayer Chapel finished?"
"We don't have the funds."
"How much is it going to cost to complete it?"
"Five thousand dollars."
"All right," said Dr. Stewart, *"Let's ask God for five thousand dollars to complete the Prayer Chapel."*

"Now, we're not going to accept any money from anyone who is here today," Dr. Stewart said, "because some of you may feel that you need to come to our rescue. The answer has to be the undeniable hand of God at work so we'll know that He has heard and answered us. Bro. James, would you lead us in prayer?" Bro. Jimmy responded:
"Dr. Stewart, I'm going to ask you to lead us if you would."
"That was Tuesday morning," recalls Jimmy Robertson. "On Thursday morning, as we were opening prayer request envelopes at the altar, my wife, Frances, came in and handed me a letter that had just arrived. It was dated the Tuesday we had prayed."

Dear Bro. Jimmy,
As my wife and I were having coffee this morning we discussed what we were going to do with $5,000 that we needed to give away. Simultaneously, we said: "We must send it to Milldale." Please take this money and put it toward the completion of the Prayer Chapel that we noticed was not

The Milldale Story

finished when we were last there. We felt that it must be due to lack of funds."

The young people, that morning, would never get over having seen the undeniable hand of God at work!

A testimony—Debbie Beasley[25]

"I have special memories of Dr. Stewart, and how he seemed to always have time for us kids. Sometimes when the other speakers and leaders of the Camp Meetings were in deep conversation over spiritual matters, he would hear us outside and would slip out to play with us. And we loved it. He was a fantastic football (soccer) player, and I remember how he could kick a soccer ball from way back, right through a basketball hoop. He made us feel special, and back then, if someone would have asked me what I thought God was like, I would have said, Dr. Stewart.

"He would walk along Milldale Road for exercise and pray for the occupants of every house he passed. Sometimes when children saw him coming they would run inside to tell their mothers that Dr. Stewart was about to pray for them."

---

[25] Daughter of Manley Beasley

Section Three

Milldale International Ministries

*We've a story to tell to the nations,
That shall turn their hearts to the right,
A story of truth and mercy,
A story of peace and light.
For the darkness shall turn to dawning,
And the dawning to noonday bright,
And Christ's great kingdom shall come to earth,
The kingdom of love and light.*[26]

---

[26] H. Ernest Nichol, 1896

12

The Greatest Task

"Go ye therefore, and teach all nations, baptizing them in the name of the Father, and of the Son, and of the Holy Ghost: teaching them to observe all things whatsoever I have commanded you: and, lo, I am with you alway, even unto the end of the world. Amen" (Matthew 28:19-21).

A Challenge from Bro. Jimmy

A message preached at the 1984 Labor Day Conference. Statistics will have changed but the need and the mandate are the same.

Folk, if your church is not involved in a world-wide ministry of reaching people with the gospel of Jesus Christ, they have no right whatsoever to claim that they are a New Testament church. You can dot every "i" and cross every "t" and boast about your theology and how straight-laced you are, but you are not a New Testament church unless you're involved in some way in world-wide evangelization. That was the commission of Jesus Christ to the church. He is still saying that to us today.

The task

The greatest task in all the world, and the one commission of the Lord Jesus Christ, is the task of evangelizing and discipling a lost world. It cost God more to evangelize the world than it did to make the world. All God had to do when He created the world was say, *"Let it be,"* and it was! He made it all out of nothing. But when God got ready to redeem the world, He became flesh and tabernacled among us. God had to die on a cross. God had to suffer and pour out His own blood to redeem a lost and dying world.

I say to you that all Heaven and Earth ought to be turned to this one purpose of evangelizing a lost, dying, and perishing world. The Word of God said that Jesus came into the world for one purpose. He healed the sick; thank God for that. He blessed and ministered to people in many areas; thank God for that. But these were all a by-product. Jesus came into the world to seek and to save those who were lost. That was His primary purpose. And He said, *"Fear not them which kill the body, but are not able to kill the soul: but rather fear him which is able to destroy both soul and body in hell"* (Matthew 10:28).

The mandate

I declare to you that none of us is more like Jesus than when we are evangelizing a world with the glorious Gospel of Jesus Christ. Everybody talks about *"Christ in you, the hope of glory,"* the very life of God being released in us and the victorious Christian life, but I say to you that if Jesus Christ takes up habitation in a man, and begins to live in and through that man, His mission will not have changed.

The Lord Jesus came to seek and to save the lost. He wept over Jerusalem. He had compassion for a lost and perishing world, and when Jesus Christ takes up habitation in us and begins to express Himself in us, I believe it will still be that compassion for the perishing multitudes because that was the purpose for which He came into the world; that was the purpose for which He shed His blood; it was for that purpose He died.

Jesus said, *"Say not ye, There are yet four months, and then cometh harvest? Behold, I say unto you, Lift up your eyes, and look on the fields; for they are white already to harvest"* (John 4:35). I want us to simply lift up our eyes for a few moments and see a world that is perishing. I'll preach this message until the entire world is evangelized. I'll preach it until every boy and girl on the face of the globe has a Gospel tract, or a Gospel of

John, or a New Testament, or a Bible in his hand. I'll preach it until every person on the globe has heard the Gospel of the Lord Jesus Christ, the news that He came to seek and to save those who are lost, and that He saves even the chiefest of sinners. I'll preach it until every tribe in India, every black face in Africa, those in China, Japan, the Philippines, and every part of the world have heard the Gospel of Jesus Christ, because I believe this is the greatest need of the hour.

Go!
Two thousand years this side of the commission of Jesus Christ in which He said, *"Go ye into all the world and preach the gospel to every creature,"* two-thirds of the world still sits in heathen darkness. Over sixty percent of the world has never heard the message of Jesus Christ. They have never heard a gospel song. Two thirds of the world own no portion of the Scripture whatsoever. I say to you that there is something drastically wrong with our method of evangelism. But there are several things I believe we can do.

Pray!
First, the Word of God declares that we can go. Second, the Word of God declares, *"Pray ye therefore the Lord of the harvest, that he will send forth laborers into his harvest."* How long has it been since you have prayed that God would send laborers for the mission field? It might be that you haven't prayed because God may send you! Everywhere I go, I hear people talking about looking for a place to preach or witness. Young preachers who have been preaching for years will say, *"I'm still looking for a place to preach,"* when two-thirds of the world hasn't heard the Gospel. I can't understand that.

When Jesus made the statement, *"Lift up your eyes and behold the harvest,"* there were 250 million people alive on this earth, but Jesus still looked at them and said, *"The fields are white."* Souls are perishing. They need to be evangelized. The early church rose up to evangelize their known world, and the Word of God declares that they turned it upside down with the gospel of Jesus Christ.

Our world

The world's population didn't reach a billion people until 1830. How much whiter was the field then? Then from 1830 to 1930, the world population doubled to two billion. From 1930 to 1970, it doubled again to four billion. By 1980, there were five billion souls alive on the face of the globe. Line the people of the world up three feet apart, and there would be souls reaching around the globe ninety-six times marching their way to a Christ-less eternity! With five billion souls, how much whiter is the harvest? I remind you that sixty percent of them have no portion of the Word of God whatsoever.

I ask you, "What's wrong with our spirit of missions? What's wrong with the evangelization of the church? How is it that we can talk so much and do so little?" Ninety million souls are being born each year, and we are reaching two million with the gospel of Jesus Christ. The world is growing eighty-eight million more pagans each year with our present rate of evangelization. You see, we're not even keeping pace by reaching two million with the gospel, when there are ninety million born each year.

The need

In 1960 the world population was 8 percent Christian. In 1970 that number had reduced to 6 percent. In 1975 there were only 2 ½ % of the world that professed to be Christians. By 1990 they tell us that the world population will be less than one percent Christian. The Word of God declares that *"the gospel is the power of God unto salvation"* (Romans 1:16). The Gospel of Jesus Christ hasn't lost its power.

The Milldale Story

India

Let me just call a couple of other things to your attention. India alone has 2,000 villages for every evangelical church. There are 778 languages in India alone. Out of those 778 languages, 26 have the Bible, 38 have the New Testament, 38 have some small portion of the Scripture, and the rest of the 778 have no portion of the Word of God whatsoever. They do not even have a gospel tract.

Indonesia

Indonesia has 838 known languages. Nine have the Bible, 19 have the New Testament, 28 have some portion of Scripture, but there are 782 languages in Indonesia that do not have a single, solitary verse of Scripture. Glory be to God, in June a year ago (1983), we were able to put one of the finest young missionary couples (Tim and Rhonda Galipeau), who were members of our church, on a plane and send them to Indonesia. There, they have buried their lives in the jungle trying to learn a pagan language so that they can translate the Word of God for them.

When we started to send them, some people said, *"I feel so sorry for them."* I answered, *"They are the most blessed people in all the world."* While we live here in our luxury, they make their sacrifices there in those jungles—glory be to God. It won't be long until it will soon be over. While most people are going to stand embarrassed at the Judgment Seat of Christ, the Galipeaus will stand tall. I tell you, while we have hoarded our money and put it in the bank, and while we've clipped our interest coupons, at the judgment, those things will not be worth the paper they're printed on! Meanwhile, the Galipeaus will have clipped theirs for an endless eternity. Glory be to God.

Columbia

Columbia has 700 languages. Three have the New Testament. Seven have some portion of the Word of God, and

50 languages have nothing whatsoever. I could give you country after country. But if these statistics don't stir your heart, I don't know what in the world will.

Can you imagine what it would be like to be born in a pagan land where many people live on less than $100 per year, and millions on $60 per year, suffering, hungry and starving? You might say, "What a tragedy and what a pity!" But I'll tell you something worse than that; they are dying without the gospel. They may never have a dose of medication to ease the pain of their body. Many have never seen a dentist for a toothache or may have never had a shot when they are dying from another disease. But I'll tell you something even worse than that; they are going to a Christless eternity where they will suffer the agonies of hell because nobody ever went to them with the gospel of Jesus Christ. Nobody cared for their souls.

Satanic darkness

Can you imagine what it would be like to be brought up in a pagan land where people are offering their babies as a sacrifice to try to appease a god that cannot be touched with their infirmities, and who cannot hear them. Many of them are being burned at stake as human sacrifices. Many drop every penny they have in some coffer to some idol god, trying to satisfy their conscience and find peace of heart that only Jesus Christ can give. The truth of the matter is that anywhere you go, on any mission field of the world, among any pagan group of people, you will find that by instinct, they know that there is a God. They know that there is a life beyond the grave. They all know it. By instinct, they know that their life hasn't pleased their god, so because of the guilt of their soul and the unrest of their heart, they turn to demons and devils, to the occult and witchcraft, and to everything in this world to obtain peace of heart, because they have never heard the good news of the gospel.

Opportunities wasted

You see, everybody is like you and me. It makes no difference if it's a little brown face in India or a black face in Africa, or a yellow face in China, they are just like we are. They feel, they have emotions, they have a heart, they have longings, they are looking for satisfaction. Ladies and gentlemen, Jesus Christ is the only One who can satisfy them. They'll never find satisfaction outside of Him.

The tragedy is that there have been doors that were open to the gospel of Jesus Christ that we failed to enter and preach the gospel when opportunity was at hand. Now, as a result, we are suffering the consequences all over the world. In 1920, in a missionary review of the world, one of the missionaries in Russia wrote an open letter that was published and circulated in America. In it, he begged for missionaries to come to Russia. He said:

"There's a great hunger in Russia for the gospel. People are turning to God by the thousands. I preach eight to ten times a day, and I'm baptizing hundreds of converts. Many out of the Russian army are turning to Jesus Christ. It is as though it is God's last call for Russia. Send us thousands of Bibles, hundreds of thousands of Bibles. Send us Gospels. Send us New Testaments. Send us missionaries." But we did not send them, and look at the consequences.

In 1924, one of the missionaries from the Orient said, *"We need 10,000 missionaries, and we need them NOW!"* The church of America turned a deaf ear. As a consequence, we sent our sons and daughters to war because we refused to evangelize.

There was a young boy who lay dying on a war field. As the chaplain stooped over him, he heard him ask, *"Why do I have to die here in these jungles? Why do I have to give my life here in this wilderness with my body blown apart?"* The chaplain said, *"The only answer I could give him was that the church of Jesus Christ failed to obey the Great Commission."*

It cost $15,000 to kill one Japanese soldier on the island of Okinawa. That $15,000, at the time, would have supported a missionary for five years on the mission field. The cost of two and a half days of World War II would have sent 10,000 missionaries to the Orient for 20 years! In 1945, General McArthur said, *"We need 1,000 missionaries."* We sent ten. In 1948, after the war, the people's faith in Shintoism was so shattered, because they had lost the war, that only 78,000 of them made their pilgrimage to worship the Sun god. When the general begged for missionaries, we refused to respond to the call. In 1950, two and a half million worshipers made their pilgrimage. In 1952, four million went. Today there is a revival of Shintoism, and they are now sending missionaries to America!

The cost of not going

There is a cost for not evangelizing. First of all, it is direct disobedience to the Word of God. Oswald J. Smith once said, *"The supreme task of the church is to evangelize the world."* I would add that the ONLY task of the church is world-wide evangelization. **We need to win folk and disciple them** so that they can win others. The reason for the existence of any church is world-wide evangelization.

As I said at the beginning of this message—if your church is not involved in a world-wide ministry of reaching people with the gospel of Jesus Christ, it has no right to claim that it is a New Testament church. You can dot every "i" and cross every "t" and boast about your theology and how straight-laced you are, but you are not a New Testament church unless you're involved in world-wide evangelization. That was the commission of Jesus Christ to the church. He is still saying that to us today.

The Milldale Story

Our strategy

I believe there are several problems. First, we just haven't gone. Secondly, our method of evangelization is often wrong. We need a God-size burden for the people to whom we go. If a missionary goes to the field and wins 75 to 100 during his lifetime, there will be a million around him who will die and go to hell. I believe if we will ever evangelize the world, it will not be done by Westerners. We need to send missionaries who will train people in their own countries to evangelize their people.

I know several missionaries who went to Mexico and trained others, and now there are 150 churches with indigenous pastors. We need to pray that in each country, God will empower missionaries to instruct and guide local men and women to evangelize their own people. It isn't just money that they need on the mission field; they need the power of God just as we need it here in America.

Milldale's mission

In 1975, God moved on my heart to do something more than just talk about missions. I'd heard messages from Dr. James A. Stewart about Russia, Bulgaria and Czechoslovakia. I'd talked to missionaries from Mexico and other places as they told about the need for the Word of God and about the suffering church that had no Bibles. I heard about the lost who didn't have a gospel tract or a New Testament. God spoke to my heart.

When God called Dr. Stewart home, I began to think about the great revival and literature ministry he had. I began to pray, and God moved upon my heart, and upon the heart of our church, to do something more about missions, so we began *Milldale International Ministries* which was dedicated to the printing of the Word of God to reach a world with the gospel of Jesus Christ.

A friend of mine was in Mexico some time back when a little Mexican woman pulled out a New Testament that was all wrapped up. When she unwrapped it, he noticed that it had been printed here at Milldale. My heart rejoices when I hear things like that.

Go with me...
Can you see us meeting with the suffering church in Russia, as a million people unwrap New Testaments that we have sent to them, piece by piece, in letter form? Can you see them studying it by candlelight? Can you picture 10,000 pulling out a Bible and unwrapping it as neighbors gather around to read that Bible, in their language, that was printed on the grounds of *Milldale International Ministries*?

Go with me to an underground church in Bulgaria where we watch a congregation pick up beautiful song books – the first to be printed in their language for 100 years. Listen as they open that song book and sing "Amazing Grace." That hymnal was printed right here at Milldale. After the song service we see them turn to a passage in a Bible that was printed here on these grounds. Then, when the pastor gets through, he goes to his study and picks up a concordance that was printed right here as well, and he prepares for the next week's message. Folk, there is no greater joy than knowing that God is using us in this way.

Go with me to Czechoslovakia and watch someone unwrapping a New Testament that was printed a few yards from where we are. We could go to Africa and find thousands and thousands of people pulling out New Testaments that were printed on these grounds. We could go to the Ivory Coast and watch hundreds of thousands picking up a piece of literature that was printed right here. We could visit Brazil's Amazon River and find hundreds and hundreds of people holding a gospel tract that would be the only scripture they'll ever know, and you had a part in printing it. We could go to China and India and find thousands of pieces of literature that went right out the back door of this little print shop.

The Milldale Story

The greatest thrill
Nothing thrills me any more than to drive up on these grounds and see an 18-wheeler backed up to the door of the print shop to pick up a load of tracts or Gospels to send around the world. I'm praying that we'll be able to reach 10 million souls a year with the Gospel. My vision has been renewed, and I'm committed to reach more souls than we've ever reached. If Jesus tarries, I want our goal to be to fill every reaching hand with the Gospel. *"For God so loved the world that he gave his only begotten Son."* Those reaching hands and perishing souls are the ones God loves! The greatest manifestation of love I know of is when we are willing to give, in order to partner in sending the gospel to a waiting and lost world.

Milldale Missions—more than just words
Rhonda Cutrer Galipeau became Jimmy Robertson's secretary and the church's pianist after she graduated from high school. Three years later, in 1976, she began her studies at Tennessee Temple College (now University) where she met and married Tim. They eventually felt called to missions, and in 1983 they were ready to be sent out by Milldale Baptist Church to Indonesia to work with New Tribes Mission. As the time approached, however, they still lacked $7500 for shipping and passage for their whole family.

Bro. Jimmy, and the Milldale Church assured them that they would take care of this need, as well as provide monthly support. So, Jimmy challenged each church member to get a "milk-carton bank" and begin saving their change during the time Tim and Rhonda continued with their deputation work.

When the Sunday arrived for the Galipeau love-offering, each family brought in their "banks," and the money was counted during the service. There were so many coins that Tim had to find a wheel barrow to carry it all to the bank. The need was met, the church rejoiced, and God was glorified!

Milldale International Ministries

Tim and Rhonda Galipeau's testimony

"Ever since 1983, when we went out as a young family to Indonesia, Milldale Baptist Church has been behind us in prayer and financial support. They were actually more than a home church to us, for we also lived on the church grounds before leaving for the field. It was fantastic to be right where everything was happening, sitting under the anointed preaching of Bro. Jimmy and being part of the Bible Conferences where we heard God speak and move hearts. We are ever grateful to Bro. Jimmy Robertson and the church for sending us out and for continuing to encourage us along the way.

"After spending sixteen years in Indonesia, we were called to train young men and women at the *New Tribes Mission's Bible and Training Center* in Northeast England. God was using our experience in tribal church planting, and other aspects of mission work, so much so, in the training of new missionaries for the field, that we assumed Indonesia was a closed chapter in our lives. But God works in surprising ways.

"In August, 2009, the Indonesian field leadership invited us to return to Indonesia to resume working with the Saluan believers on the completion of the translation of the Bible in their language. We don't feel adequate for this task, but we know that our God is able to supply everything we need. Like Bro. Jimmy says: *'Where God guides, God provides!'*"

13

The Tree Expands

Printing the Word
for the healing of the nations

*"On either side of the river was the **tree of life**, which bore twelve fruits, each tree yielding its fruit every month. The leaves of the tree were **for the healing of the nations**" (NKJV).*

When the Lord imparted a vision to the heart of Jimmy Robertson to plant a church and begin a conference ministry on Milldale Road that would touch the nation, He also gave him a heart for the mission fields of the world.

"While in prayer," recalls Bro. Jimmy, "I could hear the cry of a lost world, and I could see outstretched hands reaching for the Bread of Life. We were already supporting missionaries and mission projects with thousands of dollars, but I felt in my heart that there was more to be done, and it was not long before I realized that it was going to be through the printed page that God would use us to reach the millions.

"Dr. James A. Stewart told me how young people in countries bordering communist lands would cross the borders with Christian literature at the risk of suffering persecution, imprisonment, or maybe even death. I asked him, *'Dr. Stewart, is it difficult to get people to go, especially young people, under such circumstances?'* I'll never forget what he said, *'We have many who are willing to go, but don't have enough Bibles for them to take.'* God spoke to my heart and said: *'Milldale is going to be the place where God will provide those Bibles.'* From that day, it has been a story of miracles.

"At one point, in the early days of the ministry, we printed 500,000 Russian New Testaments to be distributed during the year the Olympics were held in Russia. This was the largest printing of Russian New Testaments up to that time. God began to open more and more effectual doors. Eighteen-wheelers were constantly hauling in paper to print and hauling literature out to the docks in New Orleans.

"I remember once, during one of our camp meetings when we were shipping out 40,000 pounds of Bibles, we took everyone out to the parking lot, and instead of a morning service we gathered around the trucks for a prayer meeting to ask God to use every piece of literature for His glory. Those were exciting days, knowing that thousands of people who had never had a copy of the Word of God would have the privilege of owning their own Bible.

"The day we put our hand to the plow, God began to work miracles. We knew that he had initiated this work, and it was evident through the years that He was in the middle of it all. And at the center of it all were two people God sent to us to manage the entire *Milldale International Ministries*—two people who would share the burden and the load, day in and day out—two people who knew how to pray and believe God. These were two of the most unselfish people I have ever known; people who were more concerned with what they could give than with what they could get, sometimes not cashing their own paychecks in order to see that the ministry kept supplying Bibles and other literature to lands they would never visit and to hundreds of thousands of people they would never meet. Ivan and Jackie Carlson are two of my most loyal and faithful friends."

A testimony—Ivan and Jackie Carlson

"Father, would you please give wisdom and direction for my life?" prayed a 28-year old electrical engineer with an aerospace company in Melbourne, Florida. Ivan Carlson had

The Milldale Story

become very dissatisfied with his work and desperately needed God's guidance. He quit his job, with no security in anyone or anything but God, and for eight months he and his wife, Jackie, sought the Lord. They had two toddlers and they had very little savings.

A life-altering encounter

"It was in May, 1972, that we attended a revival meeting in Titusville, Florida," recalls Ivan. "Bro. Manley Beasley was the evangelist. God began a deep spiritual cleansing work in our lives that consequently led to a deeper yielding of ourselves to the Lord. We told our pastor about Bro. Manley, and a few months later he invited him to come to our home church in Melbourne to minister. God mightily used him to speak to our hearts again that week. We got together with Bro. Manley for prayer and to seek God's direction for our lives.

"Bro. Manley told us about a small rural church in Zachary, Louisiana, that was much more than a church. He told us how God had created a vision for missions in the heart of a very close friend and prayer partner of his, Pastor Jimmy Robertson, and that the church was seeking God to provide someone to help direct their International Ministry and manage the printing arm of the work.

"Jackie and I began to pray about the possibility of God moving us to Louisiana to meet this need. In February, 1973, I visited their annual Bible Conference, and while there I felt a definite call of God to move my family to Zachary. Not long after that the Lord took care of the sale of our house and ten acres when our neighbor said he wanted to buy it. Within a short time we had the U-Haul loaded and were headed for Zachary. The rest is history. Jackie and I ended up serving the Lord in the printing ministry at Milldale for 25 years.

More than we bargained for...
"After settling into this new assignment God had for me, it did not take long to realize that there was more to it than I could have imagined. My "job description" would include printing, maintenance of equipment, purchasing agent, etc. The literature we printed included Christian books, tracts, a news tabloid called *Fires of Revival*, Bibles, New Testaments, Gospels of John, etc. The requests for printing Bibles, tracts, etc. were growing and Bro. Jimmy and I would often meet to pray. God was intensifying our burden to reach the world with the printed page. At that point we had a sheet-fed press, but in order to fulfill the need to print a larger volume of Bibles and other literature, we knew we were going to need a web press that would print on rolls of paper, and we found an old press in Miami, Florida. So, I traveled to Miami, disassembled the press, shipped it to Zachary, and began reassembling it on site.

"These were years of very hard work, and these were also times when we were often faced with major financial challenges that God used to grow our faith as we experienced time and again His marvelous provision and sufficiency. These times of God's miraculous provision were not lost on the children in the church, either. They were watching how the adults were responding to these challenges, and what they saw would impact their own future walk with the Lord. Bro. Jimmy's nephew, Philip Robertson,[27] was one of these children.

Childhood memories
"I specifically remember on a Sunday morning when we had a real need for paper in the printing ministry. Uncle Jimmy told the church that there was a $50,000 need for paper. They HAD to print that week. He said, 'Where God guides, He provides. We're going to pray and ask God to meet this need but we're not going to take up an offering.' As I remember,

---

[27] Pastor, Philadelphia Baptist Church, Deville, Louisiana

The Milldale Story

Mrs. Dorothy Holland stood up and sort of interrupted Uncle Jimmy at the end of the service. 'I feel impressed,' she said, 'that I am to take money that I've been saving and give it all toward this printing need.'

"She told us later that for the first time in her life she had been putting money away in savings, and that it had grown to $1500. She said she had begun to really like that money; then the Lord spoke to her heart that she was to give all of it to help buy the paper, and when she did, that opened the gate. All over the church sanctuary people spontaneously began to give.

"As a child, I didn't have any money with me that I could give, but I wrote a little pledge on a piece of paper, went forward and placed it on the altar. I wanted to be a part of what God was doing. At the end of the service, when all the money and pledges were counted, the $50,000 was there. It had come from about one hundred regular working people. There were no financially rich folk in that congregation.

"We saw God demonstrate His provision. It was one of those life-changing moments for me. Now I look back, and I see that God was using those kinds of experiences to prepare me for my ministry—years before I surrendered to preach, years before I became a pastor. Once you've experienced seeing God do that, it's easier to trust Him. So much of my ministry today is the result of the impact of what I saw God do in those days."

"We often operated on a shoestring," continues Ivan, "but with the commitment of our dedicated employees and many, many volunteers that God gave us, we persevered. Assisting Bro. Jimmy and myself were Bro. Danny Greig, Betty Causey, Iva May, Clayton Kilcrease, Jim McCaa, Rose Mary Lee, John Brown, Jerry Phillips, my wife, Jackie, and numerous others. Then there were the many youth groups that would come on weekends, and during the summer to assist in collating, binding, cutting and boxing the literature. This was not only a blessing to us, but also to them as they received a vision for the world through the printing ministry.

"Since most of the equipment we purchased was "very" used, there was always maintenance to be done on binders, stitchers, cutters, dark room equipment, plate makers, etc. Most of the projects were in foreign languages, which meant that we had to start by making negatives from a copy of the Bible or New Testament to be printed.

"We began getting so many requests for literature that we knew we were going to have to take a huge step of faith and purchase a much larger press—a brand new five-unit King web that would run thinner Bible paper. One avenue that God used to help pay for this press was through a Nashville Bible publisher. They would deliver a semi-truck load of Bible paper, and we would print for a week. Then they would bring another load of Bible paper and pick up the completed sections (signatures) of the Bible. This went on for a long time, but it aided us in getting our press paid off.

"We also held mission rallies to raise support for projects for Communist lands, and we sold Spanish and English Scriptures for the cost of materials only, which allowed us to establish a sound financial base and provided the ability to print for many countries that were under Communist rule at the time. Many containers of Scriptures were shipped to ports overseas to later be smuggled into the Communist countries.

"For more than 20 years we printed for various mission organizations, in many languages including, Russian, Bulgarian, Romanian, Spanish, Czechoslovakian, French, Portuguese, Chinese and more. On numerous occasions we were faced with printing millions of tracts and gospels for distributing organizations. Because we were operating at minimal overhead, we were able to print for these organizations at a greatly reduced cost, compared to commercial printers. *Milldale International Ministries* was also able to contribute to many of these projects through the prayerful and financial support of our own partners.

"At one point M.I.M. had 13 employees. Our presses could print 8,000 pounds of literature a day, and nothing brought greater joy to our hearts than seeing those presses running at such a terrific speed, printing the Word of God. Over the years we gave away tens of millions of pieces of literature."

Ivan and Bro. Jimmy would often take a couple of preachers with them and travel to church mission rallies to raise funds. There were numerous times, as Philip Robertson shared, that bills were due and they had no money. But God did, and He faithfully and miraculously supplied every need. They never missed a payment!

Over the years more than a billion pieces of literature in nineteen different languages, were sent out from the *printing branch* of the Milldale Tree.

14

"Send forth Thy light and Thy truth"[28]

Distributing the Word

"He sent forth his word and healed them, and delivered them from their destructions" (Psalm 107:20).

What was happening in the Milldale print shop is only part of the story. As exciting as what God was doing there, is the multitude of ways He orchestrated the distribution of the Bibles and other literature that were rolling off the presses.

On one occasion, during a period when there was a ban on religious materials being taken across the border, missionaries were transporting a truck load of Spanish literature to Mexico. The immigration officials asked to see what was in the truck, and when they opened up the back, a box fell out. When the guards looked at its contents, they couldn't figure out what they were seeing because it was in Russian, so they waved the missionaries on. The box with the Russian materials had inadvertently been put in with all the other boxes of Spanish literature, and it was the one box that fell out. Man's mistake but God's miracle!

Sonny Holland, International Evangelist and longtime associate of Jimmy Robertson, was instrumental in the distribution of a portion of what came off the Milldale presses. He shares some of his special memories.

---

[28] Psalm 43:3

The Milldale Story

The Ukraine

"With the help of our contact person in the Ukraine, we passed out many Bibles to people who traveled 50 to 100 miles to get theirs. When we had only a few left, we stopped at a little bakery to get bread. We decided to give one of the Bibles to a very elderly lady who was there, but we were not ready for her response. She fell down on the floor and started screaming and crying. She was talking, but I couldn't understand her. Our interpreter finally began relating her story to me. She had been saved right after the Bolshevik revolution in 1917, and had been praying for 60 years for God to send her a Bible. She just fell apart thanking God that she was finally holding one in her hands.

St. Petersburg

"On another occasion, Milldale International Ministries shipped 50,000 Bibles to St. Petersburg. We were to meet our contacts in a pre-determined alley, then transfer the Bibles from their truck to a bus that we had rented in Austria. From there we traveled through parts of Latvia, Lithuania and Estonia, passing out the Bibles. In one place, people gathered by the thousands. They began mobbing us because they were afraid they wouldn't get a copy. We finally had to just set the boxes out and let them grab for them.

Moscow and beyond

"In another instance, we had made contact with someone in an underground church near Moscow. It had taken three years to make proper contact because few people were able to get through in those days. We traveled by bus and met a young man at a train station about 30 miles from Moscow. He guided us to a little village where we left our bus. We walked along a train track and across a trestle before we were led into a forest. We had observed that a wagon, looking a lot like a Red Cross vehicle, had been following us. When we left our bus, the woman driver of the Red Cross-looking vehicle also got out, and now she was following us into the forest. As we walked deeper through the trees, we began to hear singing; then, to our utter amazement, we arrived at a place where about 1,500 Christians were worshiping God.

"There were no chairs, no song books, and only the pastor and a few others had Bibles. The people were standing and singing the songs of Zion. You could just sense the very presence of God. These dear Christians had to move their place of meeting every week to keep the KGB from discovering them. The Spirit of God was so strong in the meeting. Suddenly, we heard the lady who had been following us cry out, 'I'm a KGB agent, but I want the salvation you have!' We prayed with her, and she was saved. She must have been less than 30 years old. The people all followed us back to the bus where we passed out 1,500 Bibles.

"In some of the towns the people would actually fall down at our feet crying. They kissed us, hugged our feet and thanked us for the Bibles. Over the years, we took the Scriptures to Africa, Russia, including Siberia, China and Thailand— literally around the world."

When the Iron Curtain fell, it became possible to have literature printed in the Communist countries a lot cheaper because labor costs were so much less, and they didn't have the cost of thousands of dollars of freight bills to get the literature overseas. It was at this point that Milldale began to help purchase literature through local Christian ministries in the foreign countries themselves, and as a result, they felt that the purpose for which God had raised up the printing branch of *Milldale International Ministries* had been fulfilled.

They didn't want to duplicate what others were doing just in order to have a ministry, so they began to make exit plans. They still had some literature in English and Spanish which they shipped out as requests for literature were received.

The Milldale Story

Eventually, as they sold the equipment, their hearts were filled with joy to know that all over the world there were people with a copy of the Word of God that was printed right there on the grounds of Milldale. What a day that will be when those who labored so faithfully over the years get to Heaven and meet those from different lands who were saved as a result of *Milldale International Ministries.*

Jackie Carlson remembers

"During the annual camp meetings we would often carry a roll of Bible paper over to the main sanctuary, better known as "The Tabernacle," on the forklift. This was to give a visual burden so the people could believe God with us for a miracle regarding the need for more paper. God was always faithful to meet that need.

"A lot of our printing was done for the Iron Curtain countries, and these materials were carried across the borders by various mission organizations such as *Evangelism to Communist Lands,* who were involved in getting literature into those nations that were closed to the gospel. Those who were involved in that kind of ministry confirmed to us that **80% of all the literature that went behind the Iron Curtain, over a period of 20 years, was printed on the presses of** *Milldale International Ministries.*"

A special moment—Judy Scoggins

"I'll never forget when we printed a hymnal for the churches of Bulgaria. As I held that hard-bound copy of the first **Bulgarian hymnal** to be printed in over 100 years, all the print-shop workers gathered 'round to watch as I leafed through the pages. Suddenly I exclaimed: *'Oh, look! Here's,* **There is a Fountain Filled with Blood.***'* Bro. Jimmy turned to me with a shocked look on his face. *'You can read Bulgarian?'* 'No,' I said. *'But I do read music!'* We all had a good laugh, including Bro. Jimmy."

Jackie Carlson continues:

"We also printed **Haley's Bible Handbook** in Bulgarian, as well as a Portuguese devotional book for Brazil, and French literature for the Ivory Coast of Africa.

"One of the main languages was Spanish. Millions of pieces of Spanish literature left these grounds on the way to Mexico. Ed Greig and Milton Martin would fly over villages and drop bundles of the tract, ***"Dios Te Ama"*** (God Loves You). The people would run to gather them and read them. Each tract had a response card in it, and when these cards were sent in, the missionaries sent back a Bible study course to the responder. There were times that people got one of the tracts and would walk out of their village and find Ed or Milton to ask them about salvation.

"Milton Martin has shared the story many times of how a man in Mexico found a gospel tract on the ground, read it and received Jesus as his personal Savior. As a result of that tract, nearly one hundred village churches were eventually started. We don't know if that tract was printed at Milldale International Ministries; it very well could have been, but we do know how powerful the printed Word of God can be in the hands of the Holy Spirit."

15

Anyway, Anytime, Anywhere

Missionaries

Over the years God has used Milldale Baptist Church and the Camp Meeting ministry to call many missionaries into His service, to use them locally or to send them to the regions beyond with the Gospel. Several of these saints share their testimonies here.

Ed and Janell Greig
Missionaries to Mexico and Alaska
as told by Janell

"My husband, Ed Greig, along with Harold Brown and Manley Beasley, pastored churches in Nederland, Texas. They had known each other from college days, and later, when Manley went into full-time evangelism, Ed would go with him to his meetings to pray. During the days that Jimmy Robertson was praying about buying the property on Milldale Road, we got involved with the new church. We worked with the camps from the beginning along with Bro. Jimmy, Sonny Holland, Jesse Norris and Manley. After a pastorate in California, God called us to missions, and we served as missionaries sent out from Milldale Baptist Church.

"At first we stayed with our dear friends, Huey and Ocia Collier, when we were home, but when Building "B" was built, the back third of it was made into an apartment for us. Any time we could possibly manage it, we would attend the camp meetings at Milldale. I remember one time when our son John, who was about five years old, wanted to give an offering to God. I fixed an envelope for him, and he put it in the offering plate. That night, he watched as Huey and Ocia Collier, the treasurers for the church, opened envelopes to count the money. When we got home, John called me to the bedroom and asked, *"Mama, who do they think they are? God?!!"*

"Ed was a missionary pilot who worked with other missions besides *Milldale International Ministries*. He dropped tracts and Gospels of John in Spanish from the plane and performed many other services for the people of Mexico and other missionaries who needed his help. Each tract and Gospel included information about a correspondence course that could be ordered. Many people were saved as a result.

"We worked with a missionary named Milton Martin who had a six year old son who wanted to help Ed drop Gospels of John from the plane. Ed was concerned about his safety and said, *'No,'* but Milton said, *'We gave him to the Lord when he was born. Let him go.'* As Ed flew over the towns and villages, Milton's son would push the literature through a chute in the plane's floor. Before Ed realized it, the little boy had his head sticking out the chute looking around. It scared Ed to death!

"We were missionaries to Mexico for many years before God called us to Alaska for fifteen years. During all that time we thought of Milldale as being our home. When Ed passed away in 2008, he was buried in the Milldale Cemetery. We had lived by faith all through our ministry, and when Ed died I didn't know what I would do, but God has miraculously provided for me for the rest of my life."

Paul and Lolita Jones
Missionaries/Pastor

"Two of the most important and life-changing events happened to me in August, 1962. One was my conversion to a saving knowledge of our Lord and Savior, Jesus Christ, and the other was an event I attended that same month at a small country church just east of Clinton, Louisiana. The church was the Bluff Creek Baptist Church, and the conference was to be held in the parking lot under a huge tent. This turned out to be the birthing of a world-reaching ministry, born out of a vision and burden in the heart of Bro. Jimmy. This ministry would soon become known as the Milldale Baptist Church and Bible Conference Center, near Zachary, Louisiana. As a new believer, hungry for the Word, I found something at this first meeting I had never been exposed to before. The Scriptural insights and deeper life Bible expositions were to impact my life forever. I would never again be satisfied with anything less. Who would have ever thought that a place called Milldale Baptist Church and Bible Conference located in a rural area of East Baton Rouge Parish would literally impact the lives of thousands of souls over the years? I thank God upon every remembrance of that place, the God of that place, and the people of that place. Through it all, I have learned, however, that it's not the _duration_ of one's life, but the _donation_ of one's life. Or more simply put, it's not just the life we _live_, it's the life we _give_! "

Harold and Jackie Brown
Fairhaven Children's Home
as told by Jackie

"I really don't have the words to adequately express how much Frances and Bro. Jimmy have meant to me, our family, and Fairhaven Children's Home. Bro. Jimmy was not only Harold's and my pastor for many years but he has been a true yoke-fellow in the ministry. Our grown-up "Fairhaven children" still remember and talk about the blessed times they had at Milldale. Many of them were saved during the Camp Meetings.

Though Harold went to be with the Lord in 1993, through these many years we have taken care of over 900 children and now have extended our ministry to the country of Romania.

Ken and Sharon Cummings
Missionaries with HCJB

"Our relationship with Milldale goes back to 1982 when a friend of ours invited us to attend the Labor Day Conference. God spoke profoundly to us about missions, and following one of the services, we surrendered our lives to the Lord and His service.

"Our interest in using the medium of radio to reach the world with the gospel led us to working with Trans World Radio on the Island of Guam, before linking with HCJB's Global team in the Radio Planting Department, installing FM radio stations around the world in such far-away places as the islands of Dublon, Samoa, and in the country of Nigeria.

"In addition to the installing of FM stations we both were always involved in ministries through local churches, wherever we were stationed—Vacation Bible Schools, University campus ministries, ladies Bible studies, sometimes attended by the wives of government officials.

"God has blessed us in so many ways! He has protected us in times of danger. He has provided for us in times of need. We thank Him for choosing to use us, with all our inadequacies, to share His word with people around the world. And through it all, for more than 28 years, Milldale has been faithful in prayer, love gifts, vehicles, and monthly support while also allowing us to stay on the grounds when visiting area churches.

"We are now HCJB Global representatives in Central Florida, and Milldale continues to be a vital part of our global team. And just to think, it all started when God had us visit a Labor Day Camp Meeting in 1982. To God be the glory, honor and praise!"

16

"...and He gave some evangelists..."[29]

"...be watchful in all things, endure afflictions, do the work of an evangelist, fulfill your ministry (2 Timothy 4:5).

In a day when the ministry of the evangelist is on the wane in some Christian circles, Milldale has not only continued to be an encourager to evangelists, but a supporter as well. Milldale sees the evangelist as being not only divinely gifted in reaching the lost, but a catalyst for revival in the church.

Among the evangelists who have been identified with Milldale through the years is one who has partnered in ministry with Jimmy Robertson from the early days when Milldale was still but a dream. From the time God called him into evangelism, to the present, Milldale Baptist Church has been Sonny Holland's home, and this congregation has followed him with their prayers and support to every corner of the earth. The marriage between Sonny and Milldale Baptist Church stands as an example of what the relationship between itinerate ministries and the local church should be.[30]

A testimony—Sonny Holland[31]

"Dr. James Stewart was preaching on *The Heavenly Executive*[32] at the Milldale Camp Meeting. He shared about the fullness of the Holy Spirit. He said the *Heavenly Executive* came to take over if we would abandon ourselves to Him. I took

---

[29] Ephesians 4:11
[30] Additional Evangelists' testimonies in Appendix Two
[31] Sonny Holland, evangelist, has ministered on all the world's continents and as a representative of Milldale Baptist Church, has distributed hundreds of thousands of Bibles to nations closed to the gospel.
[32] The book, *The Heavenly Executive*, is available from www.revivallit.org

the keys of my life – my family, finances, and future – and gave them to the Lord. I said, *'I don't care if I don't ever preach again unless You fill me with your Holy Spirit.*

"The next day was Friday, the last day of the Camp Meeting. I had come to the meeting in a private plane, but I told the folk who owned the plane that I wasn't going to go back with them. I was determined to stay until the end of the meeting and continue to seek the Lord. I wanted to stay until God filled me with the Holy Spirit. When the others arrived in Florida, they called me and told me that as they landed in Indiantown, Florida, one of the tires blew out and if I had been on the plane, sitting in the spot where I would have been sitting, it would have probably caused a crash.

"I stayed at Milldale that Friday night and expected God to fill me with the Holy Spirit. I stayed at the altar late into the night, but nothing happened. Finally I went to the dorm, slept a while, and left the Camp Grounds. Before I left that Saturday morning, though, I prayed, *'Lord, I'm disappointed with you. I've given you everything and asked you to fill me with the Holy Spirit, but you haven't.'* I got on a commercial flight to Florida.

"At 32,000 feet in the air I was reading my Bible. I had read Galatians 4:4-6 many times. It says, *'But when the fullness of the time was come, God sent forth his Son, made of a woman, made under the law, to redeem them that were under the law, that we might receive the adoption of sons. And because ye are sons, God hath sent forth the Spirit of his Son into your hearts, crying, Abba, Father.'*

"It suddenly dawned on me that I was HOUSING the Eternal Spirit of God! He was already there, speaking volumes to me! I was filled with the Holy Spirit. The evidence of my being filled with the Holy Spirit was not an ecstatic utterance, it was instead like a fire burning right before me on the pages of the Word of God. I began weeping uncontrollably. The flight attendant wondered what was wrong with me.

"When I got off the plane, my wife Dorothy met me, and as

she looked at my countenance she exclaimed, *'Sonny, what's wrong with you?'* I explained what had happened and we wept together as we drove home.

"The next morning I preached on the ministry of the Holy Spirit. As I looked out at my congregation, those dear members of Fairlawn Baptist Church in Ft. Pierce, Florida, that body of believers I had been pastoring for the last several years, I saw them begin to fall on their knees beside their pews, weeping. Many started coming to the altar while I was preaching. I asked the Lord, *'What's happening?'* It dawned on me that when Moses came down from the mountain after speaking with the Lord, they had to veil him because of the presence of God. God was definitely at Fairlawn that morning as He manifested himself in revival, a revival that continued for months to come.

Responding to God's call

"During this period of revival I felt led to resign my salary at the church, and within a year I told my dear people that God had called me to be an evangelist. I had been reading in Genesis where God told Lot to *'Get up and get out of the city.'* That verse jumped off the page at me, and I told Dorothy that I was going to resign from the pastorate. I did so the next morning. It was like a funeral that day.

"The church was packed with people. They called Bro. Jimmy Robertson and asked him to talk with me. They wanted me to take a six-month sabbatical instead, and stay as their pastor. I told them I had to leave and go into full-time evangelism. I had to follow the will of God, not the will of man.

Starting a new chapter

"Not long after I resigned the pastorate, Bro. Jimmy, and some of his family, arrived in Ft. Pierce with a pick-up truck and a U-Haul to move us back to Louisiana. I had about $30 left in my pocket, but every bill I had in Florida was paid. I didn't owe anybody anything.

"We joined Milldale Baptist Church, and I began looking forward to my new ministry of evangelism. Since I was just starting, however, I had nothing scheduled, so I sat there waiting for God to open up the doors. I remember praying: *'Here I am, God. You called me into evangelism.'* I'll never forget His answer. *'Well, why aren't you doing it?'* I protested, *'Nobody's asking me!'* God said, *'I have!'* I got the message. I drove over to Pine Grove, a town about 35 miles away, rented a VFW Hall and had flyers made up which I distributed throughout the community.

"There were two churches in that town, a Methodist one and a Baptist one. I soon found out that neither of them wanted to have anything to do with me. Both of them were against what I was doing. There had not been a revival meeting held in that town in years. I prayed, *'Lord, if you will let just fifteen people be there, I'll preach like it's 1500!'* When I arrived at the hall that night, the parking lot was half full. By the end of the week it was packed out. People were being saved and blessed. God moved in a marvelous way. People in that area still remember that meeting. It was the beginning of my ministry of evangelism. I had become one of Milldale's first full-time evangelists!

To regions beyond

"Manley Beasley, Jesse Norris, Jimmy Robertson and I used to go to Browder's Camp in north Louisiana. In those days, people didn't have much money. We prayed about the finances for each of the Milldale camps, and we asked God for a specific amount because we believed James 4:2, *'Ye have not because ye ask not.'* Without exception, the money that came in during those camp offerings proved to be exactly what we needed. We believed that prayer can do anything God can do, and God can do anything but fail!

"Over these years, in the ministry of evangelism, in missions, and in the camps of Milldale, I have seen God move

The Milldale Story

in miraculous ways. I've seen God open doors around the world. I've seen people saved, freed in Jesus, and filled with the Holy Spirit. The message of Milldale has always been:

- Holiness,
- The Power of God over the devil
- The Fullness of the Holy Spirit
- Total Surrender.

"Our problem is not that we are out of touch with our generation. Our problem is that we are out of touch with God."
—Alan Redpath

17

"...and He gave some pastors and teachers..."[33]

"Preach the word; be instant in season, out of season; reprove, rebuke, exhort with all longsuffering and doctrine" (2 Timothy 2:2).

Many young pastors and teachers have been influenced by the ministry of Milldale Baptist Church and Camps over the years. Some were saved during the Teen Camps or Bible Conferences and later called to preach. Others responded to God's call while living on the grounds. Many young men "cut their teeth" on the strong doctrinal and biblical preaching at the camps and have rejected liberalism as a result of Milldale's influence. Three of these, who share their testimonies here, grew up in Milldale Baptist Church and have gone on to pastor growing, thriving churches of their own. Two are nephews of Jimmy Robertson, sons of two of his brothers, Ed and Louis Robertson, while the third is Manley Beasley Jr., who lived at Milldale for six of his growing up years. All three share their testimonies of how God used their upbringing at Milldale to shape their lives.

Philip Robertson[34]

When I think of my uncle, Jimmy Robertson, and the Milldale Baptist Church, 1 Corinthians 1:26-29 comes to mind.

^{26}*"For ye see your calling, brethren, how that not many wise men after the flesh, not many mighty, not many noble, are*

---

[33] Ephesians 4:11
[34] Pastor, Philadelphia Baptist Church, Deville, Louisiana

called: ^{27}But God hath chosen the foolish things of the world to confound the wise; and God hath chosen the weak things of the world to confound the things which are mighty; ^{28}And base things of the world and things which are despised, hath God chosen, yea, and things which are not, to bring to nought things that are; ^{29}That no flesh should glory in his presence."

My childhood

I grew up in a very committed Christian home, largely a result of Uncle Jimmy's testimony. He had an impact on the rest of his family—on my family! Not many kids have grown up with parents who would drive an hour each way to church every Sunday, and though they drove past many churches, they kept going because they recognized what God was doing at Milldale, and they knew how it would impact their children.

During those early years I acquired a lot of "head knowledge" about the things of God, but when I was eleven years old, during a February Bible conference when Ron Dunn was preaching, I sensed a tug of war going on in my spirit. The Holy Spirit was drawing me to Christ. That night it was crystal clear that I was lost. I went forward, and Uncle Jimmy met me at the altar. He read Revelation 3:20: *"Behold, I stand at the door, and knock: if any man hear my voice, and open the door, I will come in to him, and will sup with him, and he with me."*

Uncle Jimmy explained to me that Christ was knocking at the door of my heart, and I could be saved. I prayed, confessed my sin, asked forgiveness, and asked Jesus to come into my heart. That night, I knew He did! I was saved.

After my salvation experience, I remember something that really impacted me, and it was the story of Solomon when God said, *"I will give you anything you ask."* Solomon prayed for wisdom, but God gave him much more, since his prayer had been so unselfish. Night after night as an eleven and twelve year-old boy, I prayed for wisdom.

God's call

As a child and teenager I witnessed the reality, power, and presence of God that most people never see in their whole lifetime. It's something you never get over if you ever experience it! Uncle Jimmy always said, *"If you've ever been baptized in fire, you'll never be satisfied with smoke!"*

My high school years were pretty uneventful. As graduation drew near, however, I began to consider the call of God on my life. I knew He was calling me to preach. I remember one day when I was cutting the grass I began thinking— *"One day I may preach the gospel."*

As I began planning life after high school, I had to confront this call, and at the time I found myself rebelling against it internally. I had seen both sides of the ministry and knew it was not all glamour. I remembered the Christmas dinners when Uncle Jimmy would get a call and have to leave. I had observed him carrying more than his share of responsibility—this was not an easy life. So, I found myself turning away from God's call for the next two years as I pursued a degree that would allow me to earn a lot of money.

While majoring in pre-med at Southeastern University, I decided to volunteer to work in the Emergency Room at the Hammond, Louisiana hospital. After the first night I went home and never returned, but I still didn't run to God. Instead, I changed majors and schools. I registered at Louisiana State University in Baton Rouge and began working toward a degree in Engineering. In my sophomore year I changed my major to Petroleum Engineering, and things were going great. I had good grades and interviewed with an oil company to do an internship the following summer.

The Holy Spirit, however, was constantly dealing with me and chipping away at my resolve not to preach. The summer of 1989 became a radical turning point in my life. I finally surrendered to God's call to preach. The next hurdle was telling my family. I thought my dad would be disappointed that I had wasted two years of college.

As soon as I arrived home I told my parents. I said, *"I just want you to know that I surrendered to the ministry."* I'll never forget what happened next. The biggest smile came on my Dad's and Mom's faces. It was almost as if they knew it would happen. Dad hugged me and said, *"If you know that's what God wants you to do, nothing could make us more proud!"* We began talking that morning about my future. *"Where do I go from here?"* I called Uncle Jimmy and shared it with him. He said I should go to Bible College. He didn't suggest a particular place but said I should begin working on a Bible degree and definitely not continue to pursue engineering.

Where to go?

The first school I thought of was Louisiana College, a Baptist school where several of my friends were attending. I began making plans to head for Pineville. I even put a deposit on a dormitory room for the following fall. Manley Beasley, however, had heard about my surrender to preach and had begun to work on getting a scholarship for me at Liberty University in Lynchburg, Virginia. His kids had gone there, and he was friends with Dr. Jerry Falwell. The problem was, I had made up my mind to go to Louisiana College.

My dad and I were pressure washing our house one Tuesday morning in late summer of 1989 when the phone rang. It was Manley. *"Great news, Philip. I just got off the phone with the people at Liberty. They are going to give you a full scholarship! You just have to show up in two days."*

I didn't know what to say. Finally, I stumbled out with, *"I appreciate what you have done, Bro. Manley, but I feel like God wants me to go to Louisiana College."* I knew how hypocritical my answer was because I hadn't really prayed about it; it was just because that's where I wanted to go, but since I was talking to Bro. Manley, I wanted to sound spiritual. I knew I couldn't let him know I really hadn't prayed about it.

He must have talked ten minutes, sharing his concerns about the liberalism at Louisiana College at that time, but I'd made up my mind and essentially said, *"Thanks, but no thanks."* I realize now that part of my problem was that I had grown up on a dairy farm and had never left the state of Louisiana alone. I was a very *hometown* person. The thought of going 1,000 miles away to a college I had never seen before was influencing my thinking. I didn't want to leave my comfort zone. When our conversation ended I knew he was not pleased.

I went back to work on the house, and fifteen minutes later the phone rang again. It was Bro. Manley. This time he wanted to talk with my dad. After they had talked for about twenty minutes, Dad sat down with me and said, *"Son, you're the only one that can make this decision, but Manley is so concerned that he has spent the last fifteen minutes weeping on the phone."* That got my attention! I had so much respect for Manley. I was forced to acknowledge that his concerns were real, and I knew I had better start seeking the Lord. I was now at a point in my life that I needed to know it was really God's will and not just Bro. Manley's desires and my respect for him. I had to know for sure what God was saying, so I told my Dad that I needed to pray about it.

Timothy ears

For the first time, I did just that! *"God, if this is what you want me to do, you've got to give me some kind of confirmation – a word from You!"* As soon as that prayer rolled out of my heart, it was as if the Lord said, *"Start reading in Timothy."* I did, and in chapter one, verse three, I read, *"As I besought thee to abide still at Ephesus...."* Paul had instructed Timothy to stay at Ephesus. I put myself in Timothy's position. Paul was the one who told Timothy where to go. I turned to Titus and in verse five it said, *"For this cause I left thee in Crete...."* There it was again—the reason Timothy stayed in Crete was that Paul had told him to. God confirmed to me from His Word that Bro. Manley was my Paul. God was using him to instruct me. I knew then that I needed to go to Liberty.

To a far-off country

I had a little Toyota pickup truck, and I bought a cover for the back end, and the next morning at daylight I pulled away from home, leaving my mother bawling! Former members of Milldale Baptist Church, Ken and Gayle Taggart, opened their home in Maryville, Tennessee, to me the first night. They will never know what it meant to me to see familiar faces and receive their loving welcome.

The next morning I headed out again with Bro. Manley's words ringing in my ears, *"Find a man named Vernon Brewer, and he will help you. Find a man named Vernon Brewer and he will help you."* When I arrived on campus I asked the first person I saw where I could find Dr. Brewer. They pointed toward the administration building, and when I entered his office, I said, *"Dr. Brewer, I'm Philip Robertson. Manley Beasley sent me to you."* He stood up, extended his hand, and said, *"Oh Phil! Welcome to Liberty. We're so glad you're here."* His warm welcome confirmed that I was where God wanted me. I was given a full scholarship, and I can say that the next three years were some of the best years of my life. During that time God expanded my 'little-world' vision to a 'world-wide' one and prepared me for the ministry He had planned for me in His kingdom.

Returning home

After graduation in December, 1991, I enrolled at New Orleans Baptist Theological Seminary. I was offered the opportunity to be Minister of Youth and Music at Milldale. I was excited because it would be an opportunity to work with, and for, one of the greatest men of God I know—my uncle,

Milldale International Ministries

Jimmy Robertson. Second, I was excited about working at my home church because God had given me a vision and burden for Milldale, and I was looking forward to being a part of it.

Uncle Jimmy has unique gifts. He has a brilliant administrative mind, and being able to observe him lead a world-wide ministry with such knowledge and wisdom, made a real impression on me. I watched God intertwine administrative gifts with his day-to-day faith, as God used him to touch the world. He was a great model for me to follow.

I served at Milldale from the fall of 1992 until May 1995, and this gave me the opportunity to also work alongside some of the greatest men of God alive at that time. I developed a relationship with Bill Stafford, Sonny Holland, Bill Sturm, Ron Dunn, and many others. I led the music for the conferences, so I got to be on the platform with them. And I developed personal relationships that are ongoing to this day. Some of these men continue to minister to this day in my church.

Moving on
1995 was a true spiritual marker in my life. In January of that year I met Sandy, my future bride, at Milldale. Then, in May, when I graduated from New Orleans Baptist Seminary with a master's degree in theology, I was faced with one of the hardest decisions I have had to make—to resign from Milldale. I didn't want to leave where I had grown up and where I had seen God work so powerfully over the years.

Yet God orchestrated events over the next several months which resulted in my being called as pastor to the Philadelphia Baptist Church in Deville, Louisiana, on November 4, and Sandy's and my being married on November 25! We've been at Philadelphia ever since, and in addition to God's adding four beautiful daughters, Whitney, Lexie, Kylee and Addi to the Robertson household, we have seen God bless the church immensely as He has used the lessons I learned at Milldale to impact my ministry.

Jason Robertson[35]

Earliest memories

My earliest memories of Milldale were of the hundreds of shoes that could be seen when one lies under a pew at church. As a very young child, that was where my parents let me sleep during the long hours of the Bible Conferences. I learned that it was never good to roll over and accidently wake up under the next row. It would not be long, however, before I was sitting up, listening and watching, and being forever affected by what I witnessed.

Called to salvation

The year was 1980. I was seven years old and was sitting with my family during an evening service. I listened intently as Dr. Jerry Spencer described the realities of hell. Though I had grown up at Milldale, that night it was as if I were hearing the gospel for the first time. I had never sensed the convicting power of the Holy Spirit before, but that night I felt God's presence, and I became aware of my sinfulness while at the same time being overwhelmed by Christ's love. I knew that I needed God's redemption or else Hell was going to be my eternal future. I began to weep. Embarrassed, I bowed my head and tried to hide my tears, but my mother noticed my anguish and asked, *"What's wrong?"* I looked at her and said, *"I want to be saved."*

My mom took me by the hand and walked with me to the front row where Sonny Holland was standing. Being only seven years old, and becoming aware of my sinfulness, I felt so insignificant in the presence of this godly man, but I looked up at him and said, *"I want to be saved."* We knelt at the altar and the preacher asked me several questions to explore my understanding of the gospel. That night Christ came into my heart and I have never been the same.

---

[35] Pastor, Murrieta Community Church, Hemet, California

Called to preach

One night in June, 1985, the Milldale dining hall was uncharacteristically dark and empty. I was sitting all by myself at a table, but I wasn't alone. I could sense the presence of God, unlike anything I had ever felt since the day I first met the Lord. It was the third week of Teen Camps, and I had been wrestling with the Lord for most of that time. Being only twelve years old, I wasn't able to officially participate in the Camps, but since my dad was the Camp Chef, I was able to sneak into the worship services after I finished washing the dishes, wiping the tables, and vacuuming the floors.

I usually smelled like fried chicken at best, or dirty dish water at worst, when my chores were finished, so I had been going in the side foyer entrance to the Tabernacle where I slipped under a table that was covered with long table cloths. These provided a great place to hide my insecurities from the teenagers and a refuge from the chores of the kitchen. But what happened under those tables as I listened to the sermons set the course of my life.

It was there under those tables that God began to call me to serve Him exclusively. One night I listened to Jerry Spencer, the camp evangelist, preach on the subject of *"An Old-time Religion for the Now Generation,"* and I felt that God was calling me to reach my generation with His gospel. *"But me?"* I thought. *"I can't be used like that. Nobody will ever listen to me. I'm not even brave enough to be seen by people, much less talk to them about eternal matters."* I kept arguing with God, and by the third week of Teen Camps I found myself finishing my chores in record time and sitting on the back pew of the church wanting to hear from God more clearly. I had not slept a full night in days. I wept through every service, and I would find myself walking around the campground thinking about my life, the gospel, and the world.

The Milldale Story

Now, as I sat in the darkness of the dining hall, I was desperate. I remember foolishly demanding that God make Himself more clear to me. *"I'll do whatever You want God. I will go anywhere. I'll sacrifice everything, but I have to know what You want me to do, and I'm not leaving this room until You tell me!"* I've often thought how foolish I must have sounded to God. But God, in mercy, made His calling in my life so clear that night that I have never doubted the purpose for which I was born. Right there, God called me to preach. One year later, at the age of thirteen, I preached my first sermon!

They gave me five minutes to preach before Jerry Spencer. I looked at every face in the crowd and felt no fear. I knew God was with me. I remember glancing over at the foyer where the tables with the long table cloths were, wondering if there were any shy kids under them. I'm always looking for those kinds who have a burden to be used for God; the ones with nothing to lose, who have no other ambition but the Kingdom of God.

The heritage of Milldale

The heritage I have received from Milldale can best be expressed through the influence of the godly people I encountered there. Of all those at Milldale, the one who has had the most influence in my life is my Uncle Jimmy. He was like a spiritual father to me, giving me encouragement, admonition, advice and opportunity. I have never known a man who carried a larger burden for the Kingdom of God than he did. He has always believed that God can do mighty things with just one man who has faith.

To me, Jimmy Robertson is one of the unsung heroes of the twentieth century. He led a small congregation to trust God to do things through them that can only be explained as the miraculous workings of God, with millions of Bibles being printed and shipped all over the world, and hundreds of preachers and missionaries being called and sent from the pews of Milldale.

Milldale International Ministries

Then there were others whom God used to impact my life. Preachers like Manley Beasley, Ron Dunn, Sonny Holland, Jerry Spencer, Bill Stafford and others who have had a profound influence on my faith and ministry.

I have always been amazed at the hours these men would spend with a young guy like me. I have always tried to learn as much as I could from not only watching them preach, but also watching them live out what they preached. None of these men were perfect, but they all taught me how to live in the grace of God. They taught me the importance of repentance, and since no man of God is sinless, they taught me to be sensitive to my own sin and be quick to repent when confronted by God's Word.

Milldale has also been blessed by women of prayer. Great intercessors from Bertha Smith to Betty Martin, my childhood Sunday School teacher, taught me that no preacher will be successful if he is not supported by intercessors. Many hours were spent with such women at Milldale as we prayed for God's glory to be manifested in the churches where I was preaching. Once I was in the midst of dire circumstances on a mission trip when, all of a sudden, everything changed, and my needs were met. Later I found out that Sue Richards had risen from her sleep in the middle of the night to intercede for me as I ministered in Siberia, Russia. I discovered that she was praying at the same time the miracles were happening in my ministry.

Through the lives of all these godly people, one particular theme comes through strongly: Milldale teaches people to trust the Lord with unwavering faith. No one at Milldale will let another doubt the promises of God. Whether you were sitting under the teaching of Gordon McDaniel, or talking to one of the workers in the kitchen, or being encouraged by Ivan and Jackie Carlson, who led the printing ministry, everyone at Milldale encouraged each other to trust God and find joy in His mercies.

Milldale's lagniappe:[36] A wife!

I walked into the evening service of the 1996 Labor Day Conference at Milldale expecting to meet with the Lord. When I walked through the back door, however, the first person I saw was the most beautiful girl I had ever laid eyes on. I had met Tasha Gill six years before at a Youth Camp in Mesquite, Texas, and we had briefly dated, but this time when I saw her that night, I knew immediately that she was to be my wife. The next day I asked her to walk with me under the pecan trees near the Milldale Prayer Chapel, and as we walked, I shared my feelings with her and asked her to answer the phone if I called. She did. We fell in love and we were married within a year.

In the late 1990's my wife and I moved into the 800 square foot apartment attached to the backend of "B-dorm." We had two children at the time, Jake and Collin. During this period I served as Milldale's youth pastor and camp director. To tell the truth, I was really there to learn as much as I could from Uncle Jimmy until I knew for sure where God wanted me to go next.

The people of Milldale have always been very supportive of young ministers. Over the years they have often sacrificed to help guys like me with our tuition and housing costs. Even if they didn't meet our needs directly, preachers who have been associated with Milldale always knew that their needs were going to be met because of the prayers of the Milldale family.

Manley Beasley, Jr.[37]

My earliest memories of what would become *Milldale International Ministries* actually started with a boyhood encounter I had with the founder's son, Keith Robertson. While prayers were being offered and plans were being made that ultimately led to the purchase of a piece of property located on

---

[36] *Lagniappe:* Cajun French for something extra; added for good measure.
[37] Pastor, Hot Springs Baptist Church, Hot Springs, Arkansas

Milldale Road outside of Zachary, Louisiana, Keith and I were out back doing what boys do, which ultimately, I might add, resulted in his being injured. This also began a friendship with Keith, and a relationship with Milldale, that led to an understanding of God's call on my life for ministry.

A community of the faithful

Though my memory may not be accurate in every detail, what I do know is that the work God did in my life was a result of being surrounded by a community of faithful believers who had a passion for God and genuine revival. Our being at Milldale was not by accident because my dad felt that there was great value in raising a family where they would be influenced and supported by believers. He also felt that the best way to learn about God was to see Him work in such a way that no one could explain it humanly. As I look back, I realize that this is what Milldale was for me.

It was at Milldale that I watched God transform lives day after day, week after week, year after year. I saw Him use great instruments of revival, such as Dr. James Alexander Stewart, Major Ian Thomas, Leonard Ravenhill, and others from abroad whose names you would be familiar with. But possibly, of as great a significance, were those who may not have been as well known world-wide, but were just as powerfully used of God.

What we saw was God Almighty at work, and this was the norm rather than the exception. So many today settle for less than the manifested presence of God because they've never seen His glory revealed. Those of us who were there can never settle for "the best man has to offer" because we have seen what God can do, and there's no comparison.

It was at Milldale that I learned how to pray by watching men and women pray until the answer came. My Dad used to call this, *"praying until you have the answer in your hand or in your heart."*

The Milldale Story

It was at Milldale that I learned how to preach and to never settle for less than the anointing of God's Spirit.

It was at Milldale that I heard God's call to ministry.

It was at Milldale that I preached my first sermon.

It was at Milldale that I saw what it meant to live as a community of faith, trusting God *together* for great things. Many folk can say that they have known about someone who lived life the way God intended His people to live, but how many have had the privilege of being surrounded and mentored by these kinds of people?

Section Four

Revival and Faith

"For years we have experienced the most polished and expensive church activity in history, yet with the least dent on the sin that thrives around us. Here we are, powerless and ignored by the world. We need ten days in an Upper Room, or, maybe more suitable for us, a basement to mourn the departed Glory, and to apologize for our arrogance in preaching so long without seeing national revival." Leonard Ravenhill

18

Where does Revival Begin?
In my Heart!

"Revival is that strange and sovereign work of God in which He visits His own people—restoring, reanimating and releasing them into the fullness of His blessing."
—Stephen F. Olford

A Word from Bro. Jimmy

[12]*"And the Lord appeared to Solomon by night, and said unto him, I have heard thy prayer, and have chosen this place to myself for an house of sacrifice.* [13]*If I shut up heaven that there be no rain, or if I command the locusts to devour the land, or if I send pestilence among my people;* [14]*If my people, which are called by my name, shall humble themselves, and pray, and seek my face, and turn from their wicked ways; then will I hear from heaven, and will forgive their sin, and will heal their land"* (2 Chronicles 7:12-14).

In verses 12 and 13, God is speaking of judgment. He's saying, *"When judgment comes upon the land or upon the church, if my people will return to me, I will hear from Heaven, forgive their sins, and heal their land."* I believe that God will judge sin. In fact, I believe that the clouds of judgment are gathering over America. I don't believe that there are accidents with God. I serve a God who has all things under control. I believe that God judged Sodom and Gomorrah because of sin. He consumed it; the innocent with the guilty; the little children with the grandmothers and grandfathers. Sodom and Gomorrah had become so wicked that they brought judgment on their families and on the entire city.

I believe the hand of God has begun to judge America, and I believe there is going to be greater judgment unless God's people repent. He is going to get America's attention one way or another. We have tried to dethrone God in our country. We have basically had a godless Supreme Court. Attempts have been made to take out "under God" from our pledge of allegiance. I'm telling you, folk, we cannot defy God, turn our back on Him, blaspheme God and His Word, and not have God judge us. I believe the responsibility to see things change lies within the church.

I'm not sure that the church is in as bad a condition as we think because I believe the church may really be a lot smaller than we realize. Some people say, *"There are so many church folk who are living ungodly lives. They are just Sunday morning Christians and never get involved in what God is doing in the church. They're so unfaithful."* I'm not too sure that the true church is unfaithful. It may be that the church is just smaller than we think. It may be that **THE CHURCH** is showing up on Sunday night, Wednesday night, and for visitation. It may be that there are many whose names have been placed on our church rolls but have never been inscribed in the *Lamb's Book of Life*. I believe that God's people have a basic hunger for Him—a desire to walk with Him and to please their God.

"Return to Me and I will return to you"

We need a revival in the church today that will expose sin, wickedness, rottenness, and people's indifference. We need a revival that will call out the complacent and backslidden to a life of holiness and service for Jesus Christ. My heart is longing to see God do something in America and in our churches. Wouldn't it be wonderful if God would come in revival to your church, a revival that would be noised throughout your whole area that God is working in your church? Wouldn't it be wonderful to see the hand of God in such a way that people would come to watch you 'burn' for Jesus, where the lonely could come and find fellowship, where the brokenhearted would know of a place where they could find comfort, and where the lost would come and encounter the Lord Jesus Christ.

Wouldn't it be wonderful if it was noised abroad that Jesus was in the house, and the crowds would press in to hear Him and see Him. Present church buildings would have to become a Sunday School class, and bigger buildings would have to be built to house the people who would come because your church had become a place where the glory of God rests. That's what I'm longing for.

In our text, God is not talking about the people of the world. The homosexuals, the drug addicts, the prostitutes and the harlots are not our problem in the church. The reason for the lack of spirituality and the lack of the manifested presence of Jesus Christ lies within the church. He said, *"If my people..."* not, *"If the bar room crowd, or the ungodly bunch"* but, *"If my people... the Sunday School teachers, the deacons, the laymen of the church...If my people who are called by my name."* He's talking to those who name the name of Jesus Christ; those who would stand and say, *"I've been born of the Spirit of God;"* those who would say, *"I personally know Jesus Christ as my Lord."* He's saying if that crowd; if WE would humble ourselves. We need to humble ourselves before God.

Deity honors desperation

We are living in a proud generation. We're living in a generation that's been so blessed of God. We have so much, and we've become so self-sufficient until it's hard for us to humble ourselves and come before God in desperation. **Deity honors desperation,** and I'm convinced that if we were to become a desperate church, we would be a church that would experience revival.

Oh, that we would cry out like the Psalmist, *"My heart thirsts for God, for the living God,"* and *"My heart thirsts for God as the deer pants after the water brooks."* If we would cry out to a holy God for a supernatural manifestation of His presence in our midst, and if we would humble ourselves and see our need of God, what a difference it would make in our churches. But we're so self-sufficient and have so many programs and plans. Now, I'm not necessarily against all of that, but what we need is for God to take over our planning in such a supernatural way that we would know it was God, and He would get the glory. We can't be self-sufficient and expect God to come in revival. We have to humble ourselves before God.

The problem is, we don't humble ourselves because we don't see ourselves as all that bad. We compare ourselves with others, and we feel that we're all right. We compare our churches with other churches and say, *"We're better off than they are. We have more life and more liberty along with the preaching of the Word of God than they have."* But ladies and gentlemen, that's not the standard. Jesus Christ is the standard. The glory of God is the standard. When I stand in His presence, I see my inadequacy. I see how insufficient I am within myself, and my self-sufficiency melts before me. It makes me want to humble myself and prostrate myself before a holy God and cry out for a visitation from God in my own heart and life. *"If my people which are called by my name will humble themselves...."*

How long has it been since you have humbled yourself in repentance, prayers and fasting before God, asking Him to set your heart ablaze with the very presence of Jesus Christ? Oh, we're going to have to get desperate before God to have revival. The normal, ordinary, everyday thing is not going to get the job done. It's going to take something supernatural and extraordinary, and it's going to come to a group of people who will get desperate for God.

You know what our problem is? We're so easily satisfied with other things than with the things of God. We're satisfied with good church services, good singing and preaching. May God bring us to a place where nothing would satisfy us, nothing but Jesus and His manifested presence and His fellowship. If we would humble ourselves, we could have that.

Prayer
Next, He said, *"and pray."* This is the way for the blessings of God to come to us. He's saying *"If judgment comes, and the clouds of judgment are looming around you, it is imperative that you pray."* You may say, *"We're protected from hurricanes in our area."* But when God gets ready to judge, there is nothing that is going to protect you. God will come up with something you'll have never heard of because He WILL judge sin. If you don't remember anything else I say, remember this: **God will judge sin** – in the believer as well as in the world. We must pray! I'm talking about praying until the answer comes. I'm talking about praying through. I'm talking about praying until God comes down.

This is not the *"lay me down to sleep"* type praying, but I'm talking about intercessory prayer, the kind where your soul is so crying out to God that you don't have to make yourself pray; you'll not be able to KEEP from praying! You'll pray on the way to work, on the job, and when you get home. There'll be a constant cry in your heart for the manifested presence of God in your life and in your church. We need that kind of revival praying in the church of the Lord Jesus. We need to make up our minds that we are not going to settle for anything less than what God has for us. Most folks have sold out too cheap. We need to make up our minds that we want what God has for us, and we're not going to settle for anything less. We will pray no matter what price we have to pay in order to have the manifested presence of God on our lives and our churches.

Revival and Faith

Seek My face

God said, *"If my people which are called by my name shall humble themselves and pray and seek my face...."* Oh how we need to seek the face of God. How we need to seek the face of our Lord Jesus Christ. We need to so gaze upon His face until *"the things of earth will grow strangely dim in the light of His glory and grace."* Unless we gaze upon Him, we'll be attracted by the glitter of this world. But if we continually gaze upon the face of Jesus Christ, if we look in His face and fellowship with Him, we will realize that this world has nothing to offer us. The Bible says that the devil has come to rob, to steal, to kill, and to destroy. The devil gives the very best he has to folk in order to lure people off, and then their lives end up worse off for the rest of the way down the road. Thank God that, *"every day with Jesus is sweeter than the day before."*

If you are serving the devil, you've already had the best days you'll ever have. Yesterday was a better day than you'll have today, and it will get worse every passing day if you keep yielding yourself to the devil and keep letting him have his way in your life. It will continue to be so until you repent and get right with God, because the farther away from God you go, the worse it gets. Oh how we need to seek the face of God. We don't hear much about that anymore. You must seek the face of God and let nothing else satisfy you until you are in His presence and back in fellowship with Him.

Turn from your wicked ways

Then God said, *"And turn from their wicked ways."* Folk, there is no revival without repentance. James gives a parallel passage of Scripture in chapter 4, verses 7 through 10, *"Submit yourselves therefore to God. Resist the devil, and he will flee from you. Draw nigh to God, and he will draw nigh to you. Cleanse your hands, ye sinners; and purify your hearts, ye double minded. Be afflicted, and mourn, and weep: let your laughter be turned to mourning, and your joy to heaviness.*

Humble yourselves in the sight of the Lord, and he shall lift you up." This is the same thing 2 Chronicles 7:14 is saying. Seeking the face of God is *"drawing nigh to God."*

Then God said, *"Cleanse your hands ye sinners* (outward cleansing), *and purify your hearts* (inward cleansing). Most of you probably don't have a lot of external things people could accuse you of. That's what concerns us the most because man looks at the outward appearance. But God looks at the inside of us. That's what should concern us the most. What about your heart? Is it right with God? Is there anything in your life today that you know God is against? Is there a sin in your life? If there is, God's against it. God hates sin. Is there rebellion in your heart against God? Are you indifferent toward the things of God? Are you complacent? God hates a lukewarm Church as he said in Revelation 3:16. He said, *"I'll spew you out of my mouth."*

Are you just a lukewarm Christian, or is your heart ablaze for God? If you are lukewarm, there ought to be a returning in your heart to God in repentance and a seeking of the face of God until God rekindles the fire in your life, and you are burning for Jesus. *"Cleanse your hands ye sinners; and purify your hearts, ye double minded."* Are you double-minded and not single minded about the things of Christ? You may have some interest in the church and in God, but you're not really totally sold out to God, and this world still holds an attraction to you that robs you of a spiritual, holy walk with God.

God is demanding holiness of us. This is not a request, it is a command. God is far more interested in our being holy than He is in our being happy. God wants a holy people. Do you consider yourself a *holy* child of God? He said, *"Be ye holy, for I am holy."* In fact, the Bible says, *"Without holiness, no man shall see God."* Is there a burning desire in your heart for holiness, for purity, and for the very righteousness of God? If there's not that hunger and desire, the Bible says you'll never see God. Folk, we've watered down and whitewashed God's commands so much that they have lost their meaning. **The demands that God makes of His people are not suggestions or requests, they are demands.**

Matthew 7 says, *"Not everyone who says to me, Lord, Lord, shall enter into the kingdom, but he that doeth the will of my father."* Jesus said that too many folk are like those who build their houses on the sand, and when the storms come they have no anchor or foundation because they have not been obedient to the Word of God. God said that He would give the Spirit to those who obey Him. The reason many Christians are not filled with the Holy Ghost is that they are not willing to walk in obedience to the Word of Holy God. We must be obedient children. That's what He demands and requires of us. Until we get to that point, He cannot bless us like He wants to bless us. Instead of our being the answer to the problem, so often we are the problem itself. Oh, the glory, blessing and power we would experience if we would be sold out to Jesus Christ. Oh, the evangelization, and the manifestation of the presence and the power of God there would be on a 'sold out' church.

Notice in 2 Chronicles 7:14 where He says, *"turn from their wicked ways; then will I hear from Heaven, and forgive their sin, and heal their land."* When we think about wickedness, we usually think about adulterers, harlots, prostitutes, and gamblers, but do you know who Jesus called wicked people? He said, *"Thou wicked and unprofitable servant"* (Matthew 25:26). It was the servant who didn't properly invest his talent in the things of God and use it for the glory of God. If you're not yielded to God so that He has access to your time, your talent, your income, all you are and all you have and all you ever hope to be, you are in the category of the 'wicked and unprofitable servants.' God will take from you and invest in someone else who will invest in the kingdom of God.

I want to be a candidate whom God can invest in, bless, and use. Is there any jealousy, bitterness, or grudges in your life or church? Maybe there were past problems that you've never gotten over. You may come into the church on Sunday morning and sing the songs, but there are unresolved issues in your heart. Oh, how that grieves the working of a holy God. *"Turn from your wicked ways,"* He says. That's repentance. It's walking in one direction spiritually, then doing an about face and heading in the other direction. Then the Holy Ghost gets hold of your heart and reveals things that aren't right with God. Is there anything in your heart right now that grieves the Holy Spirit? If there is, how is He going to manifest Jesus to the congregation and convict the lost of their need of a Savior?

Why do the lost go in and out of the house of God without being saved? Often it's because the Holy Spirit is so grieved in the church that there is no conviction. Scripture says sinners can't stand in the congregation of the righteous. Let the Christians get right with God, and when sinners come into the church, they'll fall under Holy Ghost conviction and cry out, *"What must I do to be saved?"* Is there anything in your heart that's grieving God? Are you out of step with God in any area of your life? If so, why pray for revival if you're not willing to turn from your own sin and turn to God? It's one thing to say, *"I know I'm not right with God,"* and it's another thing to actually repent and turn from your wicked ways. That's when God will hear from Heaven and restore our land. I believe there needs to be a restoration in America, and God said if we, His people, would repent and turn to Him, that He will hear, forgive, and heal our land.

There is nothing in the world like having your sins forgiven. There's nothing like walking under an open Heaven. Don't argue or justify your sins, but instead, agree with God about them. Revival is when a church or person stands under the blood of Jesus with their sins forgiven and their conscience cleansed from sin. That is possible for every one of us, but the question is—***How much do we really want revival?***

A testimony—Elaine Talley[38]

"As a young girl I can remember arriving at Milldale in 1966 for the first time. The moment we stepped out of the car we felt a strong sense of God's presence on the grounds. We'll be forever grateful for the influence and teachings of Milldale; for the lessons of faith, revival, and love of Missions we saw demonstrated by men of God like Bro. Jimmy Robertson, Manley Beasley and Sonny Holland. It was at Milldale that God birthed in our hearts a **heart-cry for revival** that remains to this day. We will not be satisfied until we see God *"rend the heavens and come down"* all across this nation."

---

[38] Alexandria, Louisiana—wife of Pastor Jimmy Lee Talley.

19

Fires of Revival

Another Branch Emerges

"Return to Me," says the Lord of hosts, "and I will return to you" (Zechariah 1:3, NKJV).

In his book **Repent, or Else**, the late Vance Havner states: *"The seven churches in Asia Minor were busy, just as we are today, but to five of the seven our Lord said: 'Repent, or else.' When church membership grows statistically but church members do not grow spiritually, we have a serious problem. The greatest need of the church today is not more members, more buildings or more money. The supreme issue is not even missions or evangelism, it is **REPENTANCE and REVIVAL**. We are so busy building a bigger orchestra that we cannot stop to tune our instruments. What good is a big orchestra if two-thirds of the members never show up, or are off-key when they do perform? We are too busy chopping wood to sharpen the axe. Just as we are often too busy to have a physical check-up, so the church is often too occupied to submit to spiritual examination, yet, we never needed it more."*

The desire to publish a periodical that would focus on the Church's need of **revival** was birthed in the heart of Evangelist Jesse Norris. He had already been publishing *Revival Fires* for several years when, in 1963, he joined Jimmy Robertson in helping establish the Milldale ministry. The next year, 1964, Milldale Baptist Church took over the publication, eventually calling it *Fires of Revival,* because another organization claimed the rights to the name, *Revival Fires.*

Fires of Revival was unique among periodicals from the outset in that it had, and has, a single focus—the calling of the Church to return to her first Love, taking seriously God's admonition to return to Him. The emphasis on returning to the scriptural standard of holiness, faith and giving through the process of repentance and surrender, has not changed over the years and has been used of the Lord to awaken a desire on the part of *Fires of Revival* readers to have said of them what is written of them:

"But you are a chosen generation, a royal priesthood, a holy nation, His own special people, that you may proclaim the praises of Him who called you out of darkness into His marvelous light" (1 Peter 2:9, NKJV).

A testimony—Jerry Spencer[39]

"I was pastoring in Orlando, Florida, in the late 60's when a copy of *Fires of Revival* arrived in the mail. The terms 'fire' and 'revival' have always excited me ever since I attended a Christian college years ago. I remember the question being asked, *'Is he on fire for God?'* or *'Is she on fire for God?'* It has always been my insatiable desire to be on fire for God.

"As I glanced through the paper I saw pictures of Jimmy Robertson, Sonny Holland, James Alexander Stewart, R. G. Lee, Manley Beasley, Oswald J. Smith and others. The articles spoke of salvation, the Second Coming, the Spirit-filled life, prayer and revival. I read every word and relished every moment I spent devouring its contents.

"One of the articles was by James A. Stewart that was taken from his book, *The Heavenly Executive,* on the subject of the Holy Spirit. I ordered the book.

---

[39] Jerry Spencer, pastor/evangelist, Dothan, Alabama

The Milldale Story

"With the book came a letter from Jimmy Robertson inviting me to attend one of the Camp Meetings. I checked my calendar and discovered that I would not be able to attend any of the conferences that year but I made sure there were no conflicts for the coming year that would prevent my attending.

"It wasn't long before I received another *Fires of Revival* paper and it intensified my hunger to go to Zachary to visit Milldale, so I decided I would have to make a special trip to meet Bro. Jimmy and his family. I remember driving up from Florida, and when I got to the Baton Rouge and Zachary area, I got lost, and if you have ever tried to find Milldale you know what I mean. It's better now but back then the country roads seemed to wander all over the place.

"As I drove in the driveway of Jimmy's humble home, his two boys were playing ball. His daughter, Cathy Ruth, who is now a grandmother, was on top of the dog house with a cape tied around her neck. Her arms were stretched upward as though she was Superwoman and was about to fly. When the kids saw me, they stopped what they were doing, ran to me and greeted me as though I were an old friend. They led me inside to meet their parents. I hit it off immediately with the whole family and we've remained close through the years. And all this started with that first issue I received of *Fires of Revival!*"

Books and tapes

Fires of Revival also marketed hundreds of sermon tapes each month, and for a period of years this, along with a large discount mail order bookstore, provided enough revenue to cover all the publication costs. At one point an office was set up in Tickfaw, in the home of Bro. Jimmy's sister, Geraldine Scott, who copied the tapes, labeled them, then sent them out by the carload. Eventually, however, when evangelists and pastors began developing their own tape ministries, Milldale phased theirs out because they didn't want to be seen as being in competition.

After the fall of the Iron Curtain, Milldale's International branch began closing down the literature arm of the ministry. This meant that fewer issues of *Fires of Revival* would be printed until, in 2002, a Board of Directors was formed to help bear the spiritual and financial load. Presently, up to four issues are published annually and sent out at no charge to the reader, at a per issue cost of approximately $20,000. Many readers testify that *Fires of Revival* is a spiritual lifeline for them.

A testimony—Bill Sturm[40]

"I started pastoring in Oklahoma in my early twenties, and it was during this period that I began receiving the *Fires of Revival* paper. I would read every word of every article, and it was through the *Fires* paper that I became acquainted with preachers who had a tremendous impact on my ministry as a young pastor, and later as a full-time evangelist."

Church conferences and website

In recent years, *Fires of Revival, Inc.* has added two additional outreach branches to the ministry—Revival Conferences in churches across America, and a website. Since not everyone can attend the Milldale conferences, pastors now can have some of the same anointed Milldale Camp Meeting preachers stand behind their own pulpits and minister to their congregations. As for the website, the *Fires of Revival* paper is available for online reading, as well as news and schedules pertaining to upcoming events.

Bro. Jimmy and the board members of *Fires of Revival* are passionate about getting the message of revival before as many souls as they can because so many churches in our land are content with doing business as usual, unaware of their need. For God to come in revival, the church must be faced with the fact

---

[40] Evangelist, Valdosta, Georgia

The Milldale Story

that she has departed from Him, and for that to happen we must begin placing ourselves against the *plumb line* of God's Word.

"Amos, what do you see?" I said, *"A plumb line."* Then the Lord said: *"Behold, I am setting a plumb line in the midst of my people..."* (Amos 7:7-8).

> *It's easy to compare ourselves to others,*
> *we always come out looking pretty good;*
> *But when we place ourselves against God's plumb line,*
> *that's when we realize how far we've moved.*
> *God says, "Be holy, even as I'm holy,"*
> *so that through us His glory might be seen,*
> *And we're to be a servant unto others*
> *though it may mean that we will not be seen.*
>
> *We sing our songs, we worship every Sunday,*
> *and "I surrender all," we're quick to say*
> *Without our really thinking of repenting,*
> *can it be true we've turned so far away?*
> *We're so consumed with how we can succeed Lord*
> *that more time's spent on planning than in prayer—*
> *It's been so long since we have known your power*
> *that we don't miss you when You are not there.*
>
> *We're like a wall, a wall's that leaning,*
> *our hearts have turned and we have gone astray.*
> *We're like a wall, a wall that's leaning,*
> *Lord, may your plumb line draw us back to You today.*[41]

---

[41] Words from the song, *God's Plumb line*, by Ron and Patricia Owens

20

What is Faith?
(part one)

"Faith is the rope that binds our nothingness to God's almightiness."
—*Jimmy Robertson*

If there were a defining word for Milldale's ministry over the last, almost five decades, it would be the word, **faith.** Not only was it preached, not only was it talked about, but it was practiced. From the moment God began to impress Jimmy Robertson with His vision, he knew that there was no way for the vision to be realized through his own efforts; it was going to have to be God's doing. He knew that God was not only the *Vision-Giver,* but He was the *Vision-Fulfiller.* Bro. Jimmy knew that now, his full-time assignment was going to be cooperating with God in His business.

Years before people were exposed to Henry Blackaby's teaching about *"joining God in what He is doing,"* Bro. Jimmy was working that principle out in his own experience. He knew that not only did God have to plant the tree, but it was God's work to grow the tree into maturity. Bro. Jimmy's part was to believe, **in faith,** that God was doing it and to join Him in the process.

And so, Jimmy Robertson began asking himself the question: **"What is faith?"** He knew it had to be more than what he saw happening in the churches around him. He knew it had to be more than what he was seeing practiced in the lives of many pastors and their people. He wanted to learn and practice biblical faith, the kind of faith that pleases God.

A testimony—Ken Fryer[42]

"No one can be intimately associated with Milldale, and Brother Jimmy, and not understand the role that faith plays in the ministry. This fact was illustrated to me in 2002, when Jimmy walked into the office and said, *'Son, I believe that the Lord wants me to invite Jim Cymbala to preach in the next Bible Conference.'* I am embarrassed to say that my first thought was—*'There's no way Bro. Jimmy's going to get Jim Cymbala, pastor of the Brooklyn Tabernacle, to come to Milldale.'*

"Brother Jimmy dictated a letter to his secretary, Judy Scoggins, and sent it off to Pastor Cymbala. A week later, Pastor Cymbala's assistant called Brother Jimmy and scheduled a phone conference with him. When the appointed day came, I remember how all of the staff crowded into Brother Jimmy's office to listen in on the conversation. When it was over, Jim Cymbala had agreed to come preach at Milldale!

"On the opening night of that Bible conference, after the opening music, Brother Jimmy exclaimed, *'I tell you, we're having a camp meeting, not a cramp meeting!'* When Pastor Cymbala preached, the Spirit of the Lord moved in a mighty way."

A Word from Bro. Jimmy

Hebrews 11:6 says: *"He that cometh to God must believe that he is, and that he is a rewarder of them that diligently seek him."* There are several scriptures that remind us that without faith it is impossible to please God. If that is so, it is important that we know what that means so we can check up on ourselves to see if we are living the kind of faith life that pleases God. A good place to start will be Joshua 14:6-12.

---

[42] Senior pastor, First Baptist Church, Greenwood, Louisiana

Revival and Faith

The basis of faith
⁶*Then the children of Judah came unto Joshua in Gilgal: and Caleb the son of Jephunneh the Kenezite said to him, Thou knowest the thing that the Lord said unto Moses the man of God concerning me and thee in Kadesh-barnea.*

⁷*Forty years old was I when Moses the servant of the Lord sent me to Kadesh-Barnea to spy out the land: and I brought him word again as it was in my heart.*

⁸*Nevertheless my brethren that went up with me made the heart of the people melt: but I wholly followed the Lord my God.*

⁹*And Moses sware that day, saying, Surely the land whereon thy feet have trodden shall be thine inheritance, and thy children's forever, because thou hast wholly followed the Lord my God.*

¹⁰*And now, behold, the Lord hath kept me alive, as he said, these forty and five years, even since the Lord spoke this word unto Moses, while the children of Israel wandered in the wilderness: and now, lo, I am this day fourscore and five years old.*

¹¹*As yet I am strong this day as I was in the day that Moses sent me: as my strength was then, even so is my strength now, for war, both to go out, and to come in.*

¹²*Now therefore give me this mountain, whereof the Lord spake in that day; for thou heardest in that day how the Anakims were there, and that the cities were great and fenced: if so be the Lord will be with me, then I shall be able to drive them out, as the Lord said."*

Notice the basis of Caleb's faith. *"Thou knowest what the Lord said concerning me and thee."* Forty years before, God said to Joshua and to Moses that every inch of ground Caleb's feet would trod upon, would be his. Caleb believed it, and though he spent forty years wandering in the wilderness with a crowd that wasn't going anywhere, Caleb never forgot where he was going! He was headed to the land of promise. He knew it and he believed it. He had the promise; the title-deed was in his heart; the substance was in his heart because **faith IS substance.** He knew, because God had said that the land he would trod upon was going to be his.

God's Word

God's Word is always the basis of our faith. Bible faith is not faith in our faith; it's **faith in the Word of God and His faithfulness.** Caleb said: *"I want that mountain,"* not because it's going to belong to me, but because it does belong to me. God had spoken to Caleb when they had spied out the land and he and Joshua had returned with a good report. The rest of the spies returned with an evil report because they looked at it from a natural standpoint, but Caleb and Joshua saw it from God's perspective.

From the "top side" they saw the land as their land. All the others were looking at it from the "bottom side." The doubters said: *"There are giants and walled cities."* Caleb and Joshua said: *"Let's go in and take the land at once. God has given it to us."* Why were they so confident? Because their faith was based on what God had said. This is where true faith is based, not on our opinions or ideas.

When the Holy Ghost takes the Word of God and communicates the promises of God to our hearts, the written Word becomes the living Word, and we can stand on it and die on it, knowing that it is a reality to us.

There was a secret between Caleb, Moses, Joshua and God. They knew something the rest of Israel didn't know. They knew the land had been given to them by God. *"Thou knowest what the Lord said concerning me and thee."* Knowing what God has said about a situation will enable you to walk through valleys, face giants, and go through the storms.

In 1963, when a group of fifteen folk and I started Milldale Baptist Church, I had one thing in my heart. I didn't have a dime of money, we didn't have any land, I didn't have a salary but I had one thing—I had the promises of God. Nobody underwrote us, but God did, and it was better to have the promises of God than it would have been to have more material possessions because **His promises are always sufficient.**

A friend of mine, Manley Beasley, tells about something that happened to him in the early days of his ministry. A man came to him and said: *"I want to underwrite your ministry so you will be free to go and preach, and you'll be able to depend on me for your support."*

"I can't do that," said Bro. Manley. *"You may not have enough to underwrite my ministry." "I have a million dollars,"* the man said. *"That's good,"* replied Bro. Manley, *"but what if I need two million? I have the promise of God which is the assurance of all I'll ever need in my ministry."*

Manley Beasley's faith was based on God's Word, the promise that God had communicated to his heart when He said: *"I will never leave thee nor forsake thee"* (Hebrews 13:5). Manley believed God when He said: *"My grace is sufficient for thee"* (2 Corinthians 12:9) and when He promised, *'I will supply your need according to my riches in glory"* (Philippians 4:19). **Faith must be based on the Word of God.**

Today, what most people call faith is nothing but nonsense—this business of *name it and claim it,* just name and claim whatever you want. The only thing that we are to name and claim is that which God has spoken, not what the flesh lusts after. Most folk who name it and claim it seldom are doing it for anybody else, it's for themselves—for personal things.

You hear television preachers say: *"Plant some seed faith, send your offerings in and next month you'll get rich, but be sure to get your offering in right away because we have to have it before the end of the month."* What I wonder is, why in the world don't they give what they have as seed faith and believe God that He will adequately meet all their needs? No, while many of them heap money into their own coffers and become rich and build kingdoms for themselves, they prey on ignorant folk who don't know the Bible, and on poor folk who want to get rich.

This kind of gospel is appealing to people because it promises health and wealth. They're told, *"You won't have any pain."* Well, nobody wants to hurt or be sick. They're promised that they'll get rich if they'll do this or that. This is a "prosperity gospel" that is born in hell! Some of the greatest saints of God I've ever known have been sick and poor, but yet have an all sufficiency in God. From their hospital beds or bedridden in their homes for years, they give more praise and honor to Jesus than most folk, and their lives are filled with the glory of God. They just trust Him day by day and find all their sufficiency in Him. God is adequate for them! Many in the charismatic world, however, would say, *"If they'd get right with God they'd get well and be rich."*

From despair to victory

Some years ago I was in a meeting in Phoenix, Arizona, where I preached on faith one morning. An intelligent, attractive young lady with a college degree came to me at the close of the service to ask if Frances and I and the pastor would have lunch with her. At lunch she told us the following story.

"My grandfather was ill, and some friends told me that if I would just believe God for his healing that God was obligated to heal him or He would be a liar. I began believing for his healing and confessing to everybody, 'My grandfather is healed,' but he kept getting worse. I went back to the Scriptures they had given me, (Scriptures they had taken out of context) and I kept confessing them. He kept going downhill—then about a year ago he died. I had believed so much in what they had told me that I kept on confessing his healing and believing that God would resurrect him.

"We had a funeral service, went to the grave, and when they started to lower the casket I asked the funeral director to open it up. He didn't want to, and at first the family refused, but because I was so persistent he opened it. I looked into the casket and said: 'In the name of Jesus, get up.' I was humiliated and embarrassed. The faith I had had in the past was shipwrecked. Since then I haven't been able to pray or trust God for a single thing. But when I heard you preach this morning I knew where I went wrong. I listened to what others proclaimed and I heard absolutely nothing from God."

Taking God at His Word

Faith is simply taking God at His word. When God communicates a truth to your heart by the Holy Spirit, and it becomes reality and an assurance to you, that faith is the title deed to the things you're asking God for. Let me quote Bro. Manley again—***"Faith is acting like something is so when it's not so in order for it to be so because God says it is so!"***

When I began the ministry God told us to start with fifteen people, I had already received some promises from God. What I was doing was not my idea, and I sure was glad I had not thought it up because there were many times when I had to go back to God and say, *"God, this was not my idea. I wasn't the one who started this. God this is your responsibility.* If God puts you in the middle of something, it's His responsibility. Now, if you start something yourself and end up in a mess, you'll suffer the consequences. But if you're following God and you find yourself in a storm, you can rest on one thing—God is in the middle of the storm with you. Faith comes by hearing—hearing the Word of God.

Faith—the only approach to God

The carnal Christian walks by sight. The spiritual man walks by faith, not on the basis of what he sees, hears or touches, but on the basis of what God has said. Often there won't be any feelings in the faith walk. Sometimes when we're trusting God He has to detach us from feelings to find out if we're walking by feelings or by faith.

Faith is human weakness laying hold of God's divine strength.
Faith is your invitation to God to use you on His terms.
Without faith, we see what man can do. With faith, we see what God can do—that's why we need to live the faith life.

Without faith we might do a lot, but it won't last. We may get excited about something for awhile, but as soon as the excitement is gone, we have to come up with something else to excite us. But, when we're living by faith we can climb over the mountains and walk through the valleys. Faith takes the few loaves and fishes and feeds a multitude. Faith calms the stormy waters or gives you grace to shout in the midst of the storm! One is just as good as the other. Faith can do the impossible!

21

What is Faith?
(part two)

"Faithful is he that calleth you who also will do it" (1 Thess. 5:24)

*Faith is the substance of what you are looking for
before it has even arrived.
God says it, that settles it, so go act upon it,
and you'll have a faith that's alive.
To get in on what God has promised His children
depends on some action from you.
A faith that is living means more than just trusting,
It's doing what God says to do.*[43]

A Word from Bro. Jimmy

An island encounter

I remember an occasion when Sonny Holland, Manley Beasley and I went to an old camp my brother Ray had on an island on Lake Manchac. It had a grove of Bald Cypress trees—**trees with knees!**

It was about ten days before a Milldale Camp Meeting, and we were facing several challenges. We decided that we needed to *fast and pray* for a week. One of these challenges was financial. We had expanded some of our buildings, charged the materials, bought groceries for the Camp Meeting on credit, and

---

[43] From the theme song that was used on Manley Beasley's radio program, *Living Faith*. Words by Ron Owens.

had 90 days to pay these bills. We did this knowing that God had quickened our hearts to believe Him for the supply. We never doubted and were looking forward to seeing His glory.

We prayed, we studied Scripture, we read some good biographies, we stayed before God for a week. On the last day we decided that the three of us would take our Bibles and a pen and pad and go in different directions and write down what we believed the Holy Spirit was saying to us about the things we were seeking answers for. We wrote down what we were trusting God for in attendance, what we were trusting God for spiritually, and what we were trusting God for financially.

When my brother returned to pick us up in his boat that afternoon, we were still in that Cypress grove praying. Manley Beasley was the first person to arrive back at the camp, and Ray asked,

"Where are Jimmy and Sonny?"
"They'll be back in a bit," Manley answered. *"We've been out seeking the mind of the Lord so that when we leave the island we'll know for certain that the financial and spiritual needs of the church and camp have been met, and what God wants us to trust him for."*

Ray said: *"Let me see what you wrote down."* Manley handed it to him. About that time Sonny and I both walked up and handed Ray our sheets of paper. When he compared the sheets, he discovered that we had all written down exactly the same things and had given the same verses of Scripture.

The offering

When the offering was taken at the close of that last Camp Meeting service, Bro. Manley got up and said: *"Praise God for..."* and he told the congregation the amount that was in the offering, the same figure that God had given us out on the island. The amount was so large that the people were staggered.

The money was already in, but it had not been counted yet. Someone called out to Bro. Manley:

"You know, I don't think it is possible to have that much money in the offering with this crowd. I'd like you to count it." There's always a doubter around!

Bro. Manley told the ushers to take the offering to the dining room in building "C." We all went and started counting. All the checks, all the big bills, all the middle size bills, the little bills on down to the half dollars, quarters, dimes, nickels and pennies. There were about a dozen people, most of them "unbelievers," standing along the wall watching as we counted. And while we did, we were rejoicing and praising the Lord.

When they laid the last penny on the stack, the total came to exactly the amount we had written down out there on the island, and the amount Bro. Manley had announced there was in the offering. Now, did that mean we were great? No! It meant that we had a great God! It just proved the faithfulness of God to His Word. Our faith wasn't in our faith; our faith was in the Word of God that He had quickened to our hearts.

The Bible says that *"if any two shall agree"*—glory to God, there were three of us agreeing because we believed that God had spoken to our hearts. This wasn't a matter of reaching up into thin air, it was a matter of hearing from God! *"Faith cometh by hearing!"* That's the way it goes, folk. **Faith is the title deed to all the resources of God!**

Another test
Several of us were in Sulphur, Louisiana, in a revival with Joe Prather when I got word from the office that more bills had come in, including a note that was due. I began to fast and pray about this need and the Lord spoke to my heart that the money would be there when we got back to Milldale on Monday. I told

Manley and Sonny what the Lord had shown me. Manley looked at me and said: *"You believe that?"* I said, *"I sure do."*

"All right," said Manley. *"Call Bro. Joe Young* (Milldale's treasurer), *and tell him that you'll have the money to pay the note on Monday when we get back. Tell him to announce it to the church at the Wednesday night prayer meeting so they can praise God that the money has come in, because faith is reality, and if God spoke to you, what He said is reality—it is done."*

Well, I picked up the phone and said: *"Joe, we have the money to pay the debt. Tell the church that I'll have it on Monday."* Nothing happened on Thursday. Nothing had come in Friday evening when I got home. Saturday morning I got up with blessed assurance. Soon it was time for the mail-run. I called the children in and said, *"Today there is going to be $4000.00 in the mail. Which one of you wants to get it?"* I forget which one brought it in.

We began to open the envelopes. There were a few contributions to the Camp ministry—$5.00 here and $10.00 there. I'll never forget it. James was real young at the time, and he looked at me and said: *"Daddy, the money's coming. It's just a little bit at a time."* I looked at the envelopes that were left and knew that there were not enough left for it to come in that way. Then we opened one of the last envelopes. The check inside was for $4000.00, the exact amount we were praying for.

My mother-in-law was visiting us at that time. She had never seen God perform a miracle like that. When she left she went all over the country telling people how God supernaturally worked to perform that miracle. God is a supernatural God. He is a God of miracles!

To budget or not to budget?

We limit God so often. Bro. Danny Greig and I were recently talking about church budgets and how many times they are based on human calculations. The problem with this is that we are teaching people to walk by sight. We're teaching them to walk by what they can see. I'm not against church budgets, but what I'm saying is that if we begin by analyzing the congregation's resources and planning a budget by what we can see, then all we'll know is what **we** can do. But if a church budget is planned on the basis of what the will of God is, I tell you, it will be far bigger and you'll have far more than you ever thought you would have in the treasury of your church.

Through the years we never had a budget at Milldale Baptist Church because the needs for ministries varied so much from day to day. We knew, and I would remind the people that no matter how big the need was, God had more than enough to meet it. We believed that where God guides, He provides. All we need to know is that we are following the unseen hand of a holy God. We'd step out over and over again with financial needs that were staggering, and we did that because God had spoken. We would say,

"God, this is your idea, you initiated it. God it is in your hands. It's your ministry and we trust you to pay the bills."

I confess that I've been brought down a few times and wavered some. I'm no hero. There were times we faced a crisis when it looked like there was no way out. I would then have to abandon myself to God and tell Him that I didn't have the ability to raise the kind of funds that we needed. I had to roll the responsibility over on God, and He never failed to provide for everything He initiated.

Elijah hears from God

Remember when Elijah was on Mt. Carmel? Remember what he prayed? *"Let it be known this day that thou art God in Israel, and that I am thy servant, and that I have done all these according to thy Word"* (1 Kings 18:36). He didn't just decide one day that it was time for God to chastise Ahab. He didn't tell Ahab that he was going to ask God to withhold rain for three and a half years. No! God had told Elijah what He was going to do—that He was going to send a drought in the land in order to

The Milldale Story

judge the king and Israel for their sin, and that Elijah was to meet Ahab *'in the way'* to tell him what God was about to do. When they met, Ahab asked Elijah, *"Are you he that troubleth Israel?"(1 Kings 18:17.)* *"No,"* replied Elijah. *"I'm not the one troubling Israel. I'm just the messenger boy sent to tell you what is going to happen"* (paraphrase). Elijah had received a Word from God.

THERE!

Remember what happened later? God told Elijah to go down to the brook, Kidron, and that He would feed him there. I like that! God said, *"I'll feed you THERE!"* Elijah could have been anywhere else in the world, and the ravens would not have shown up. But he was THERE, where God had told him to be, and folk, if you are THERE where God tells you to be, His blessings will be on your life because God will be THERE!

Let me tell you, when things start getting low; when finances begin getting tight, I start asking, *"Am I there?"* Am I doing what God wants me to do? Was it His voice I heard? You'd better be sure you are there when the brook dries up like it did for Elijah.

The next place God sent him was to a bankrupt widow. All she had was a little oil and a little meal (flour). I know Elijah must have been a Baptist preacher because he told the widow to bake him a cake FIRST; just like a Baptist evangelist would do. She did. She baked the man of God a cake, and then to her surprise, she didn't run out of oil or meal. Every day there was just enough. You know why? Because God had said to Elijah: *"Go to the widow's house."*

I expect that Elijah would have felt a lot better if the Lord had told him that he was to go to the banker's house in town. Or, *"I want you to go to the Real Estate man's house, or the rancher's place."* No. God said: *"Go to the bankrupt widow's house."* God wanted Elijah to have to trust Him every day, day after day.

Now, back to what Elijah said to God when he was on Mount Carmel, with Ahab and all his priests. "I've done all this according to thy Word." In other words:

"God, I didn't think this up. This is not my plan. I wouldn't have the sense to figure this all out. You were the One who initiated this. Now, Father, so that everybody around will know that this is your doing, send the fire."

And the fire fell! Now, someone else may try the same thing, and there will be no fire because they didn't hear from God. They're not able to say, *"I've done this according to thy Word."*

Finally, the faith we're talking about is faith that is based on the revelation and illumination of the Word of God to our heart. It is not thumbing through the Bible and putting your finger on a verse and claiming it as a promise. No. It's finding out what God is saying in your situation and, I tell you, when you do, you'll discover that God is faithful!

Don't try to have faith in your faith. In my younger days I used to do that. I'd pray, then look to see if I had enough faith. I'd look at it and say, *"I'm not sure if I have enough faith so I'm going to go back and pray again."* Now, I'm not against praying a hundred times, but my prayer must be based on the faithfulness of God and not on my faith. God must be the object of our faith, not our own faith. I've got news for you. It isn't the amount of faith that counts, it's the choice of faith. It's choosing to believe God.

Faith is living in obedience to God's divine plan, purpose, and will. If you are living the faith life, your life will not always be explainable. That's the thrilling thing. That's when God gets the glory, the Lord is magnified and glorified. When people ask what makes you tick, you can say, **'God!'"**

The Milldale Story

*It's not enough just to say you believe it
if you don't intend to obey.
God has so clearly revealed in His Word
how He wants us to live every day
You'll find that you don't have to wait until heav'n
to get in on what God has for you;
As you dare to step out in faith you'll discover
what God says He'll do, He will do!*[44]

---

[44] From *Living Faith,* by Ron Owens

22

A Prince Has Been Taken From Among Us

*Throughout the years of ministry there have been several preachers identified with Milldale who walked as closely with Jimmy Robertson as anyone could walk—preachers who have personified what Milldale has stood for—men of **faith and revival**. Several of these are written about elsewhere in this account of the Milldale story, but there is one who warrants special attention—a preacher known and deeply loved by the many his life touched. A preacher who still shadows the Milldale campground.*

A tribute by Jimmy Robertson on the occasion of the home-going of Brother Jesse Norris

We're here today to praise God and to celebrate the life and home-going of my friend, Bro. Jesse Norris. Some people would say that a prince has died among us, but I prefer to say that a prince has not died, but a prince has been lifted out from among us.

I want to reflect on our brother's life by tying it to what the Apostle Paul wrote in 2 Timothy 4:1-8,

[1] I charge thee therefore, before God and the Lord Jesus Christ, who shall judge the quick and the dead at his appearing and his kingdom; [2] Preach the Word; be instant in season, out of season; reprove, rebuke, exhort with all longsuffering and doctrine. [3] For the time will come when they will not endure sound doctrine; but after their own lusts shall they heap to themselves teachers, having itching ears; [4] And they shall turn away their ears from the truth, and shall be turned unto fables.

The Milldale Story

⁵But watch thou in all things, endure afflictions, do the work of an evangelist, make full proof of thy ministry. ⁶For I am now ready to be offered, and the time of my departure is at hand. ⁷I have fought a good fight, I have finished my course, I have kept the faith: ⁸Henceforth there is laid up for me a crown of righteousness, which the Lord, the righteous judge, shall give me at that day, and not to me only, but unto all them also that love his appearing.

Paul is speaking here about a soldier, a warrior. He says, *"I have fought the good fight, I have kept the faith."* When I look at Bro. Jesse's life I am looking at a soldier who fought a good fight. **He was courageous in conflict and victorious in battle.** The reason he was victorious was that, as the Scriptures declare, he didn't entangle himself with the affairs of this present life.

He didn't entangle himself…

Paul said, *"For to me to live is Christ and to die is gain."* This could be said of Bro. Jesse whom I have known for 50 years. And in those 50 years I have never known him to take a fishing pole and go fishing. I've never known him to go out in the woods to hunt. I've never known him to go golfing. I'm not saying that there is anything wrong with any of these, but there won't be any rewards for those activities. Bro. Jesse was constantly spending his time on things of eternal value—on things that mattered. He never got involved in political debates, and the few times I was around him when that was happening, I remember him saying: *"Brethren, let's pray!"*

For him, to live was Christ. That's why he was a good soldier. Pastors, wouldn't it be wonderful if all of us would be like Bro. Jesse who was **single-hearted and never faint-hearted because he was never double-minded.** How often we get so entangled that we fail to be a faithful soldier of the Lord Jesus.

Revival and Faith

He was a good soldier.

Bro. Jesse was never half-hearted because he was wholehearted for God. It could be said of him that he wholly followed the Lord. And I'm saying that of a man who was in the ministry for over 60 years and who preached over 15,000 sermons. Glory to God! He kept a record of every place he preached and every sermon he preached and what God did in every church he was in. That's how important being a good soldier of the Lord Jesus Christ was to him.

He was courageous in conflict.

Bro. Jesse was courageous in conflict. He was a conqueror. He fought the fight of faith in every situation. He fought the fight for purity, the purity of the Word of God. He believed *The Book!* He believed and preached what is in this book.

But not only did he preach it, he lived it. **He believed in and fought for purity in the Christian life. He believed in holiness.** He preached holiness. You don't hear much about that anymore. And not only did he preach it, but he lived a holy life. Bro. Jesse was a gentleman, and there was never an accusation made against the moral fiber and character of his life. Think of that—after sixty years in the ministry. Today this kind of life doesn't seem to mean that much anymore, but it did to Bro. Jesse. He knew he was going to have to guard his life and keep it pure if he was going to be a good soldier of the Lord Jesus. Oh that all of us would follow the example that our brother set in his life of purity.

He had a charted course.

Bro. Jesse had a charted course. He knew why he was born. He knew where he was going, and he set his face in that direction, and all his life he pursued that for which he was born. He didn't run all over the place, in this direction and that direction. He had set his course, and he never wavered. That course was to preach the Word of God and to serve the Lord

The Milldale Story

faithfully. He kept that goal in view, and he never took his eyes off of Jesus. He pressed on in the battle as a good soldier and he would often admonish others to *press on*. *"Press on,"* he would say. *"Press on, press on, press on!"*

How often he has said that to me because he wanted me to cross the finish line in faith and victory. Bro. Jesse had a charted course and he kept pressing on toward its destination. How important it is for a preacher to know why he was born; to know where he is going, and to live as though he believed it and not be tossed about by every wind of doctrine. So many are constantly trying to come up with something new and different rather than preaching the old and proven truths of this Word, and letting God change the lives of the hearers. Bro. Jesse had a charted course.

He believed in a Spirit-filled life.

Not only did Bro. Jesse have a charted course, but he believed that to keep going on that course he had to live a Spirit-filled life. Through all his years of ministry, Bro. Jesse always recognized the *other Evangelist*—the Holy Spirit. He knew **He** was the real Evangelist. He knew the real preacher is the Holy Spirit. He knew that we are just the instruments God's Spirit works through.

I remember the first time I heard him preach. At the end of his message he said: *"If anyone here wants to be filled with the Holy Spirit, come to the altar."* He didn't believe that being filled with the Spirit was a one-time experience but that it is a life totally yielded to God and controlled by Him, and that this is something we need to daily be checking on.

Now, I've been a Baptist all of my life, but I tell you, I believe that the Bible teaches that you have to be filled with the Holy Ghost if you're going to be a faithful soldier of the Lord Jesus. The reason Bro. Jesse preached with the anointing of the Holy Spirit, the reason he preached with such power and authority, was that he was filled and controlled by the Spirit of God.

A lot of preachers would like to be able to preach with the anointing and power of a Jesse Norris, but that kind of living and preaching comes with a cost. It is like something that Bro. Ron Dunn said to me one time about Bro. Manley Beasley. He said: *"Pastor, I would like to have what Manley has, but I have to be honest—I don't know if I'm willing to pay the price that he has had to pay."*

I believe that that kind of Spirit-filled life and anointing is available to every man of God if we are willing to pay the price. Bro. Manley used to say: *"You can have as much of God as you are willing to pay the price for."* Jesse Norris was willing to pay the price because he knew why he was born, and he knew where he was going. He had a charted course and he was empowered by the Holy Spirit.

He had a contemplated crown.

The Apostle Paul said in verse 8 that: *"There is laid up for me a crown of righteousness which the righteous judge shall give me in that day and not to me only, but to all them that love his appearing."* You know what happened when Bro. Jesse died? He was freed from everything in this life that he had no desire for. Paul said that to live is Christ and to die is gain. Bro. Jesse was freed from sin. He was freed from doubts. He was freed from temptation. He was freed from his enemies. He was freed from suffering. He suffered in those latter years, but he suffers no more. And think of it. Death freed him from death. There are no graves on heaven's hillsides.

He has a soul-winner's crown.

I believe Bro. Jesse not only has **a crown of righteousness** but he has a **soul-winner's crown**. He was a soul-winner. He loved souls. If there is one indisputable thing about our brother, that would be his love. He loved people, he loved his God, and I don't know anyone who loved the church of Jesus Christ any more than Bro. Jesse did. He looked forward to joining that part of the body of Christ that was already in heaven, and with them, to lay the crowns that are given to him at the feet of his Lord.

Oh, won't it be a great day for Bro. Jesse when, at the throne of God, he is surrounded by those he has won to Jesus in all those little country churches, those big city churches, along with the souls from foreign lands. Can you hear them saying? *"Thank you for loving me, Bro. Jesse. Thank you for caring enough to bring the gospel to me. Thank you for praying."*

He was a prayer warrior

This is one area where Bro. Jesse is going to be mightily missed. We've lost a prayer warrior. There are few people I've known who knew how to pray as he did. You know why he was victorious in battle? He knew where the battle was fought. **He knew that all victories are won in the prayer closet.** He knew that what happened in revivals, in the churches, in the lives of people were but the spoils of the battle that had been won on his knees. Bro. Jesse was a man of intense prayer up until the day God took him home. He'll be missed! He prayed daily for me and my family. He prayed for the ministry for over 40 years—every day, every day, every day. I will miss him.

May the example of Bro. Jesse's life, and what God did through him, not be lost on us. May we set our course and not faint in pressing on as faithful soldiers of the King, never forgetting that the spoils we pick up in our ministries are but the result of battles already fought and won on our knees. May God keep raising up pastors, evangelists, faithful warriors in every walk of life who press on with their whole heart.

A prince has been taken from among us, but he will not be forgotten. He will live on through the thousands of souls who were saved and the hundreds of preachers who have been called into the ministry through this faithful soldier of the cross, our friend and our brother, Jesse Norris.

Interlude

Giants Walked These Grounds

Through the years, leaders of the world-wide evangelical community made their way to those 16 acres on Milldale Road in East Baton Rouge Parish, some to be guest speakers at the Camp Meetings, while others felt led to permanently take up residence and become part of the on-going ministry. To give honor where honor is due, and to give glory to God who orchestrated the yearly speaker rostrum for the Camp Meetings, a brief sketch now follows of but a few who, already having passed on to their reward, stood behind the Milldale Tabernacle pulpit. An account of others, such as James Alexander Stewart and Jesse Norris, are found elsewhere in the book.

Manley Beasley[45]

"Faith is believing something is so, when it is not so, in order for it to be so, because God says it is so."

Little did Bro. Manley realize that, when God brought Ed Greig and Harold Brown into his life while they were still in college, their relationship would one day lead all three families to Milldale.

Discovering a oneness in spirit with Jimmy Robertson and the vision God had given him to establish a Camp Meeting and Conference ministry, the three walked with him through the years as this vision unfolded. Though they were all different, they had one thing in common—a total commitment to the Lord Jesus, and the fulfilling of His mandate for their lives. Though these three, who started out together, have now gone on to their

---

[45] The biography, *Manley Beasley: Man of Faith, Instrument of Revival*, is available from Milldale Baptist Church or www.beasleybiography.com

The Milldale Story

reward, the impact of their lives is still being felt.

"*Bro. Manley,*" as articulated by his brother-in-law and fellow evangelist, Mike Gilchrest, "*had a heart that was set on glorifying God in his flesh and his union with Jesus. It was like a marriage intimacy and relationship that was so unique it was almost mystical. It was for better or for worse, in sickness and in health, until death took him into the presence of his Lord.*"

Jimmy Robertson describes the first time he had Manley in a meeting. "*After the service, he announced that we were going to stay at the church to pray. We prayed until 1 AM. Next morning at 5 o'clock I heard a knock on my door and there stood Manley. I said: 'Is there an emergency? He said: 'There sure is. We need to pray.' We went back to the church and prayed until noon. That was the beginning of a great revival in our church and community.*

"*During the six years the Beasleys lived at Milldale, and I served as their pastor, Bro. Manley was my teacher. He taught me many things, but the two most important things were about faith and prayer. I learned what he meant when he said that, 'You either have the answer in your hand or in your heart'.*"

As effective as Bro. Manley's ministry was prior to his becoming ill with three terminal diseases, his greater ministry was during the twenty years of sickness when he was in and out of Intensive Care, and the only explanation for his being alive was that he was being kept alive by the life of Christ.

The friendships established at Milldale continued and deepened to the very last day of his life. The spiritual bonding with Bro. Jimmy, Sonny Holland, Jesse Norris, Ed Greig and others was such that, when he knew God would soon be calling him home, he returned to his Milldale friends for one final visit.

Bro. Manley's spiritual legacy will live on through subsequent generations as those he touched pass on the truths he taught and modeled while he lived among us.

Interlude

Curtis McCarley

Jimmy Robertson: "Curtis McCarley was one of the greatest Bible expositors and one of the most holy, praying men I've ever known. God used him in the mid 50's and early 60's across the south in a mighty way. After we started the Milldale Bible Conferences, Curtis McCarley preached for us in two or three conferences every year until his untimely death in 1973.

"This left a void difficult to fill and it was at this point that I invited Ron Dunn to speak at the next February Conference where Bro. Curtis was to have ministered. God immediately bonded the hearts of Ron and Kaye Dunn with the Milldale family, and Ron would eventually speak at every subsequent February Conference until his own "home-going".

Ron Dunn

Ron Dunn lived, preached, and taught what I call "muscular Christianity." He had been in the trenches and fought the battles, and he knew what it meant to meet the enemy head-on and live by faith. He offers no "three easy steps" to victory nor does he peddle simplistic prescriptions for joy and peace. If you want muscular Christianity that glorifies Christ and builds character, then you want the practical Bible ministry of Ron Dunn." —Warren Wiersbe

Many tributes have been written about this son of Poteau, Arkansas, who became one of Milldale's favorite perennial speakers. He began preaching at the age of fifteen and before his death in June, 2001, he had preached in churches and Bible conferences in many parts of the world. He was a lover of horses, simple food, target shooting, the family farm in Greenwood, Arkansas, and his toy poodle dog, Belshazzar. Adrian Rogers nicknamed Ron, "Chief Yellow Horse" because of his Cherokee heritage. Ron went on to become one of the English-speaking evangelical world's favorite preachers.

"Ron Dunn was one of the most gifted men of our generation in rightly dividing the Word," recalls Jimmy Robertson. *"His messages were profound and yet simple. They were well illustrated with personal application. Ron's messages and books were so Christ-filled that they will live until Jesus comes."*[46]

Jimmy Draper remembers Ron as being one of God's truly unique preachers. *"Gifted with a keen mind and a focused heart, Ron Dunn gleaned diamonds from the mines of Scripture and held them out for examination in a way that is unforgettable."*

Kaye Dunn Robinson remembers

"Ron's first time to preach at Milldale was at the February, 1974 camp meeting. This would be the beginning of 25 consecutive years of Milldale ministry, with one exception—the year he wrote down the wrong date."

Front pew conversation, Monday evening, February conference:
Jimmy Robertson: *"Danny, have you heard from Ron Dunn?"*
Danny Greig: *"Not recently. But he usually walks in about this time."*
A few minutes later. *"It's almost time for him to preach. Why don't you ask Jackie to try to reach him by phone. Perhaps something has happened."*

"Hello, Ron?"
"Yes."
"This is Jackie Carlson from Milldale. We were wondering..."
"Oh my. Is this the week I'm supposed to be with you? I must have put down the wrong date. I'm so sorry. I'm in a meeting in San Antonio...."

---

[46] Ron's books available from www.sherwoodbaptist.net/bookstore

Interlude

"Milldale was just about Ron's favorite place to go," continues Kaye. "He always said that they were 'his kind of people.' I believe part of what he meant was that every year he found himself with preachers who were doing what God called them to do. There were not always big names, there were no special accolades or pastors from "fancy" churches, but just men who loved the Lord with an extravagant faith. We always expected God to work at Milldale because the meetings were bathed in prayer, and there was always an expectancy that God was going to do something special.

"We never arrived early because we usually got lost trying to find the place. We always walked in on Monday night as they were singing, and you could just feel the anticipation! We were always welcomed with open arms and were so thrilled to be there. As I look back, it's hard to believe that God did such marvelous things in such an obscure place hidden way out in the country. The fellowship with Jimmy Robertson, Bro. Manley, Danny and Sonny was something Ron relished year after year.

"We'd marvel as we listened to the reports of the miraculous things God had been doing with the printing and distribution of Bibles and other Christian literature around the world, the Teen Camps or the conferences held each year. And then there was Frances Robertson's cooking! She always made Ron either a banana or coconut pie. And of course, being with Brother Manley was icing on the cake as Ron's heart beat as one with his.

"I recall there being more outward expression at Milldale than we'd see in our other meetings. There was no hesitancy in letting out a good shout or a loud, *Amen!* yet we rarely felt it was out of place. Ron and Bro. Jimmy were about the only ones who never seemed to show much outward expression, but this didn't mean they weren't full and running over on the inside—it just wasn't their personality.

"I remember one year when we were so packed out that we were stacked in all the way down to the platform. Bro. Manley was preaching but was so weak that he had to sit in a recliner. At one point he said something that set one brother off, and he came running down to the front, praising the Lord. He ran straight through our packed-in group, then back to his seat and never stepped on a single toe. That was a miracle in itself. Ron said he sensed it was in the spirit; it didn't distract Bro. Manley, who went on with his message.

"Some of the best preaching was done by people you had never heard of. Bro. Jimmy would ask men to speak, as he felt led, in those morning meetings. It was fun to watch some of those younger preachers grow each year and become outstanding pulpiteers.

"Milldale has been *a place of meeting,* an Ebenezer for many pilgrims. I thank God for the special memories I have of those times spent with our precious friends."

Oswald J. Smith

It is thought by many that there may not have been a greater missionary statesman since the Apostle Paul, than the Canadian, Oswald J. Smith.

Pastor, evangelist, missionary statesman, author, hymn writer, poet, editor, world traveler, Oswald J. Smith, born in 1889, was one of the most versatile Christian leaders in the history of the Christian church. Perhaps never has one man done so many different things well. Much of his ministry centered in Toronto, Ontario, where he founded *The Peoples' Church* that he pastored from 1933 to 1959. During those years he raised some $14,000,000 for foreign missions, more than any other pastor in history to that time. After he turned the pastorate over to his son Paul, to become pastor emeritus and missionary at large, the church has continued to send out and support thousands of missionaries over the years.

Interlude

Dr. Smith's travels took him around the world, and though suffering from ill health most of his life, he persevered. After almost dying on one of his trips, someone asked him; *"Why, when you are so weak, do you spend so much time and energy doing what you do?"* His one-sentence response, that originated with him, would become world-famous: *"Why should anyone hear the Gospel twice before everyone has heard it once?"*

Among other quotes that allegedly originated with him are:

"Give according to your income lest God make your income according to your giving."
"The church that ceases to be evangelistic will soon cease to be evangelical."
"It's not how much of my money will I give to God, but, how much of God's money will I keep for myself."

Oswald Smith preached his first sermon in 1908. Some 12,000 sermons later, he preached his last one in December, 1981, at the age of 92, in the church he had founded in 1933, *The Peoples' Church,* Toronto. He slipped away at the age of 96 to fully experience what he had written many years before:

I have seen Him, I have known Him,
for He deigns to walk with me;
And the glory of His presence will be mine eternally.
O the glory of His presence, O the beauty of His face,
I am His and His forever, He has won me by His grace.

Dr. Smith's funeral was held on Thursday, January 30, 1986, at the *Peoples Church.* George Beverly Shea sang. Billy Graham preached.

Leonard Ravenhill

"If Jesus had preached the same message many ministers preach today, He would never have been crucified."

Leonard Ravenhill was a British evangelist/revivalist best known for challenging the modern, backsliding church to return to God. Everywhere he went he called Christians to repentance, believing that until the church humbled herself before her Maker, there would be no revival. Through his teaching and books, he addressed the disparities between the New Testament Church and the Church in our time.

In his early years, before moving to the United States in 1959, his meetings drew very large crowds in Britain, resulting in many converts devoting themselves to Christian service at home and abroad. Many Christian leaders attribute their calling and their understanding of the Christian walk to Leonard Ravenhill. He was a close friend of A. W. Tozer who said of him, *"To such men as this, the church owes a debt too heavy to pay."*

He and his wife, Martha, lived at Milldale for several years during which time he preached from the Camp Meeting pulpit on many occasions. He was known for his ability to express truth in a very succinct fashion and was one of the most quoted "revivalists" of his generation.

Roy Hession

"To concentrate on service and activity for God, may often thwart our attaining of the true goal, God Himself."

Roy Hession was born in London in 1908, and became a Believer in 1926, through the witness of a cousin who was a navy officer. After working for a Merchant Bank for ten years, he committed himself to fulltime preaching and became one of the most effective Christian evangelists in post World War II Britain, especially among young people.

His understanding of the Christian life underwent a radical change in 1947 following a conference that he had arranged. He had invited members of the *East Africa Revival Movement* and was very much influenced by their strong emphasis on a personal implementation of the basics of the Christian faith and the healing powers of transparency and repentance in particular. In the years that followed, Dr. Hession ministered to many churches and conferences in Europe, Brazil, Indonesia, Africa and North America and preached on several occasions at Milldale.

His books continue to be sold and read worldwide. His first book, *Calvary Road*, written in 1950, has been in print in English ever since. His last book, *Good News For Bad People*, was finished in 1989 just hours before he suffered a serious stroke. One, or more, of Roy's books has been translated into more than 80 languages.

This servant of God went to be with his Lord in 1992. He'll be remembered by the thousands his life touched over the years and for his unwavering stand on the principles of repentance and grace that had become so precious to him.

R. G. Lee

"We live in a world of invertebrate theology, jellyfish morality, seesaw religion, India rubber convictions, somersault philosophy and a psychology that tells us what we already know, in words which we do not understand."

R.G. Lee was born November 11, 1886. The midwife attending his birth held baby Lee in her black arms while dancing a jig around the room, saying, "Praise God! The Lord has sent a preacher to this house." A God-sent preacher well describes Dr. Lee who pastored Bellevue Baptist Church in

The Milldale Story

Memphis, Tennessee, from December, 1927 until April 10, 1960. During those years over twenty-four thousand people joined the church, with over seventy-six hundred of these for baptism. Dr. Lee preached his famous sermon, *Pay Day Someday,* over 1200 times in the United States and overseas.

He was born into a poor, but deeply religious sharecropper family in Fort Mill, SC, and early in life felt the call to be a preacher. In spite of many obstacles, he heeded that call and went on to win many scholastic and oratory honors in his University and eventually earned a Ph. D. in International law from the Chicago Law School. But more significant than all of these was his ordination that took place in his boyhood church, First Baptist of Fort Mill, South Carolina, in 1910.

From his humble birth to sharecropper parents, Dr. Lee rose to not only pastor one of the largest churches in his denomination but to serve the Southern Baptist Convention as its president for three terms.

After his retirement he preached for 18 more years in churches small and large, in conventions great and small. Milldale was blessed to have had this special servant of God stand behind the Tabernacle pulpit on several occasions before God took him home in 1978. He was 92.

Duncan Campbell

"True revival is a move of God that affects not only church members, but the surrounding community in a way that is visible to all parties concerned."

Duncan Campbell was a fiery Scottish preacher known as the primary spiritual leader in the Lewis Awakening, or Hebrides Revival in Scotland's Hebrides Islands from 1949-1952.

Interlude

He was born in 1898, in the Scottish Highlands, and came to faith through members of the Faith Mission in 1913. After military service during the First World War he trained with the Faith Mission, and served with them for a number of years, mainly in the Highlands and the Islands of Scotland, including the Island of Skye. He was well suited for this as he was a native Gaelic speaker.

In 1949, after having been gone for 25 years, he returned to Skye, traveling back and forth from Edinburgh by motorcycle. His ministry was greatly blessed of the Lord as he saw many people being converted to Christ. Then, in the midst of this ministry, he received a call to go to the Island of Lewis in the Outer Hebrides, a call he initially resisted, but when the doors began to close in Skye, he felt that his was a sign that he was to go to Lewis.

The call came from a pastor, James Murray MacKay, at the prompting of two Gaelic-speaking sisters in their eighties who had been praying for revival for years. It was actually on the third invitation that Duncan Campbell accepted, and almost immediately upon his arrival a move of God began with men and women calling on God and turning to Him. He planned to stay for only two weeks but ended up spending the next two years on the Isle of Lewis where he experienced a mighty outpouring of God's Spirit in revival as he traveled from village to village preaching repentance and grace. Many were converted during those days.

While speaking at a *Faith Mission Conference* in Northern Ireland, and in spite of his being expected to speak the next day, he felt that he was to go immediately to the island of Berneray. Not knowing anyone there, and not expecting anyone to know him, he was met at the dock by an elder of the local church. This church was without a pastor, and this elder, who had been interceding for his island for months, became so convinced that Duncan Campbell would be coming to Berneray, that he had begun announcing meetings where Duncan Campbell would be

The Milldale Story

preaching. The rest is history as the flames of revival reached to every corner of that island and very few were left untouched by the power of God.

Duncan Campbell was outspoken about the work of the Holy Spirit. He believed that *true revival* is a move of God that affects not only church members, but the surrounding community as well. It is something that is visible to all parties concerned, prompting such things as the closing of bars, along with a significant decrease in crime. He also knew, from firsthand experience, that revival begins on our knees.

Duncan Campbell went to be with his Lord in 1972, not long after he had walked the grounds of Milldale where he had once again witnessed the glory of God.

Section Five

No Turning Back

"Brethren, I count not myself to have apprehended, but this one thing I do, forgetting those things which are behind, and reaching forth unto those things which are before, I press toward the mark for the prize of the high calling of God in Christ Jesus."
—Philippians 3:13-14

23

Take the Land!

"The reason so few Christians are optimistic is that they have a misty optic."—Vance Havner

A testimony—Jeremy Pruitt[47]

"In February of 2000, the Lord began to take me on a remarkable journey which began on the grounds of Milldale Baptist Church. This camp has profoundly affected my life and ministry. I consider myself blessed beyond measure to have attended the conferences these last ten years.

"Milldale has been my seminary. There has never been a time when I attended that God didn't speak to my heart. Every pastor, evangelist, ministry staff member, layman and their spouse, would do well to get in on what God is doing here! Henry Blackaby said it best: *"Look for where God is working and join Him!"* God is working at Milldale! It is a spiritual oasis in a dry and thirsty land!"

A Word from Bro. Jimmy

I want us to take a look at the children of Israel at the time when they spied out the land of Canaan. We know the background of the story. We know how Moses appointed the spies who would go in and how they reported back that they had found everything exactly like God said it would be. They had found cities; they had found fruit—grapes, pomegranates, and figs. This land that God said that He would give them was a wonderful and glorious land. We read about it in Numbers 13:25 through chapter 14:9.

---

[47] Pastor, New Beginnings Fellowship Baptist, Sulphur Springs, Texas

²⁵*And they returned from searching of the land after forty days.*
²⁶*And they went and came to Moses, and to Aaron, and to all the congregation of the children of Israel, unto the wilderness of Paran, to Kadesh; and brought back word unto them, and unto all the congregation, and shewed them the fruit of the land.*
²⁷*And they told him, and said, We came unto the land whither thou sentest us, and surely it floweth with milk and honey; and this is the fruit of it.*
²⁸*Nevertheless the people be strong that dwell in the land, and the cities are walled, and very great: and moreover we saw the children of Anak there.*
²⁹*The Amalekites dwell in the land of the south: and the Hittites, and the Jebusites, and the Amorites, dwell in the mountains: and the Canaanites dwell by the sea, and by the coast of Jordan.*
³⁰*And Caleb stilled the people before Moses, and said, Let us go up at once, and possess it; for we are well able to overcome it.*
³¹*But the men that went up with him said, We be not able to go up against the people; for they are stronger than we.*
³²*And they brought up an evil report of the land which they had searched unto the children of Israel, saying, The land, through which we have gone to search it, is a land that eateth up the inhabitants thereof; and all the people that we saw in it are men of a great stature.*
³³*And there we saw the giants, the sons of Anak, which come of the giants: and we were in our own sight as grasshoppers, and so we were in their sight.*

14 *And all the congregation lifted up their voice, and cried; and the people wept that night.*
²*And all the children of Israel murmured against Moses and against Aaron: and the whole congregation said unto them, Would God that we had died in the land of Egypt! or would God we had died in this wilderness!*

The Milldale Story

³And wherefore hath the Lord brought us unto this land, to fall by the sword, that our wives and our children should be a prey? Were it not better for us to return into Egypt?
⁴And they said one to another, Let us make a captain, and let us return into Egypt.
⁵Then Moses and Aaron fell on their faces before all the assembly of the congregation of the children of Israel.
⁶And Joshua the son of Nun, and Caleb the son of Jephunneh, which were of them that searched the land, rent their clothes:
⁷and they spake unto all the company of the children of Israel, saying, The land, which we passed through to search it, is an exceeding good land.
⁸If the Lord delight in us, then he will bring us into this land, and give it to us; a land which floweth with milk and honey.
⁹Only rebel not ye against the Lord, neither fear ye the people of the land; for they are bread for us: their defense is departed from them, and the Lord is with us: fear them not.

The "ables" and the "not ables"

It was an amazing thing how, when all of these folk went in to spy out the land, two came back and said, *"It's a great land. Let's go in and take it,"* while the rest of them said, *"It's a great land, but we're not able to take it."* Here we have the "ables" and the "not ables." Notice verse 30: *"And Caleb stilled the people before Moses, and said, Let us go up at once, and possess it; for we are well **able** to overcome it."* Then we have verse 31, *"But the men that went up with him said, We are **not able** to go up against the people; for they are stronger than we are."*

We still have those same two categories today. There will always be the "well able" and the "not able" folk in every church. There are people of faith and people of unbelief. When the spies who went into the land came back to report to the children of Israel, both groups gave the report that the land was a good land, exactly like God said. It was a land flowing with milk and honey. Both said there were giants there, and walled cities, but the largest group said, *"We are not able to overcome it."* This says one thing to me—**the majority is not always right!**

This majority said, *"We are not able to overcome,"* and basically, they committed a sin unto death because of the fact that they would never enter into the land of Canaan because of their unbelief. The others said, *"We are well able."* We see here that Caleb had a different spirit. There is the spirit of unbelief in the hearts and lives of so many people today, and this spirit of unbelief always sees the worst in everything. They see the big giants and the walled cities. They see everything as impossible.

Those, however, who say, *"We are well able,"* look at circumstances from a different viewpoint. They see life from God's viewpoint. The trouble with those spies who said, *"We are not able,"* was that they looked around and saw everything in sight, but they never saw Him who is invisible, the One who is able to do all things!

We are going to look at a few things about Caleb and Joshua. We're going to look at their courage, what they saw, and we're going to look at the reason they were successful in life and why they entered into the land of Canaan. We're going to see that we're either going to enter in, or we are going to wander in the wilderness. That's the truth!

Staying put, or entering in?

There are people in every church who are not going anywhere. They're just wandering about in circles, hoping something good happens. But basically, because of unbelief they are never willing to attempt the impossible. When anything comes up in the church, they are the ones who say, *"We can't. It's an impossibility. It's too difficult. Look at the cost. Look at our finances. Look at the labor that will be involved. We are **not able** to do it."* Do you know anybody like that in your church?

Then you have those who are the **"well able"** folk. They

don't operate in ignorance. They see the problems and they see that there are difficulties. They know that it will come with great sacrifice, but they say, *"We are able to do it because God's in it. We can do it because of the promises of God."*

It must be a terrible thing to live in unbelief, to always see the negative and never see the positive. **Some folk can never see the positive in anything because they don't ever see God in anything.** I remember a man one time who nearly fell out with me because I had recommended some things to the church that were nearly impossible. He said, *"I just don't see it."* I didn't say it publicly, but when we got out of the meeting, he told me again; *"I don't see it."* I said, *"I can tell you why you don't see it; you're blind."* He got upset with me. I said, *"You're the one who said you can't see it. Now who is it who can't see and is blind?"* That's why some folk can't ever see what needs to be done. They can't ever see the plan and the program of the church. They are spiritually blind. *"I just can't see it,"* they say. Well, if you're like that, you need to have your eyes anointed.

Caleb and Joshua had courage. They saw that there were giants, but they said, *"Those giants are bread for us."* They said, *"Let's go in and take the land."* But you know what the children of Israel did? They believed a lie when they listened to the spies who said, *"We can't go in and take the land. There are too many giants. The cities are too difficult. We can't take the land."* They believed a lie because they could not embrace the promises of God and operate on what God said.

To me, it's amazing how a preacher can get up and preach his heart out, preach the truth, expound the Word of God, and somebody in the church who has never walked with God can begin to sow seeds of doubt and unbelief, and the people will follow him. Rather than following the man of God and relying on the promises of the Word of God, they will believe the devil's lie and not do anything.

These Israelites didn't want to do anything. They said,

"We'd be better off going back to Egypt or just dying out here in the wilderness." You know what the difference is between them and me? I'd take my chance if I were going to die anyway. It's like the lepers at the gate when the Assyrians had their camp set up and the city under siege. The leprous men said, *"If we go in the city we're going to starve to death. Live or die, sink or swim, we're going into the Assyrian camp where the food is! We're not going to just sit here."*

It's surprising how many people in the church are content to just sit there. They have no interest whatever in taking the land and conquering for the cause of Christ. They are blinded to the promises of God and the reality of the work of the Holy Spirit. They believe the devil's lies and say, *"We can't."*

But Caleb and Joshua said, *"We can. Let's go in and take it at once. Let's not wait. Let's not put it off."* I believe they were looking at the promises of God, and bless God, they would have started to march that night if the people would have gone with them. They would have gone in and would have taken the land. But no, the people began to criticize and say, *"Let's stone Moses; let's stone Aaron. These preachers have brought us out here, and now we're going to die following them."* But if they would have followed them they could have gone into the land flowing with milk and honey. But they said, *"Let's set us up some captains to lead us back to Egypt."* It's amazing how some folk want to set up their "captains" in the church—captains who often are unbelievers and doubters.

From God's perspective

We notice from watching Caleb and Joshua that they saw things from God's perspective. They said, *"They are larger than us."* But how small were they in God's sight? They were looking at it from God's viewpoint. No problem is too big for God. Did it ever occur to you that God has never had a big problem? God has never been impressed with big men.

Caleb and Joshua saw it from the top side, and that's where

we need to be looking because we are seated with the Lord Jesus in the heavenlies, looking at every situation from the top side—seeing it as God sees it.

I'll tell you, it looked a lot different to God than it did to those unbelieving spies! Caleb said, *"They are larger, but they are going to be bread for us."* The unbelievers saw opposition that would be death to them, but Caleb and Joshua saw it as being a blessing to them. *"Bread is for our nourishment!"* Caleb said, *"Those giants will do nothing but nourish our faith. They're going to be what will strengthen us. Those giants are going to witness the supernatural activity of God because we're not looking at ourselves, we're standing on the promises of God, and God said, 'I'm going to give you the land.'*

The truth of the matter is that God had already given it to them. When they got to Rahab's house, she said, *"Forty years ago, God had given you the land."* Joshua 2:9-11 says: *"And she said unto the men, I know that the Lord hath given you the land, and that your terror is fallen upon us, and that all the inhabitants of the land faint because of you.*
[10]For we have heard how the Lord dried up the water of the Red Sea for you, when ye came out of Egypt; and what ye did unto the two kings of the Amorites, that were on the other side Jordan, Sihon and Og, whom ye utterly destroyed.
[11]And as soon as we had heard these things, our hearts did melt, neither did there remain any more courage in any man, because of you: for the Lord your God, he is God in heaven above, and in earth beneath."

Here was a pagan woman who had more faith in God than all the Israelites who had seen all the miracles. She said, *"We heard what God was doing for you, how that God was fighting your battles, and the people's hearts melted. There was no spirit left in them to fight. They had already given up."* You know what happened to Israel? They marched right back into the wilderness when those in Canaan had already given up. Rahab said that there was no spirit in them to fight, and that they had no courage. They knew God was fighting for Israel.

Folk, Rahab knew something. She knew that God was undertaking for the children of Israel. She was seeing it from the top side. It's amazing. She was a harlot woman. Of course, Bro. Curtis McCarley said she had already left the harlot business and had gone into the weaving business because she was stacking the flax on the roof getting ready to go to work. There had already been a change in her life!

Caleb and Joshua knew that they were going to grow because of the problems they would face in the land. You say, *"There are so many problems in the church."* Well, thank God for them. If you respond to them right, you'll grow up.

Problems are never really the problem. The reason God designs our problems is not to change our circumstances, but to change us in our circumstances.

What God is wanting to do is to change us. That's why He creates problems in our lives in the first place. He wants to let us see what is in us; how we will react to the problems, and whether or not we have faith in God.

The title deed is yours!
Caleb and Joshua saw the situation from the viewpoint of God's promises. They said, *"The Lord is with us."* There was a smile on their faces and they had the deed to the land in their pockets. He had already given them the land and victory. The whole time the Israelites were marching in the wilderness, dying like flies because of their unbelief, with the judgment of God on them because they had stood against the promises of God, Caleb and Joshua were never fearing death. While the rest of them were wandering around, dying, Caleb and Joshua were going somewhere—they were headed toward the land that was flowing with milk and honey. They knew that it would one day be theirs.

The Milldale Story

When Caleb was 80 years old, he said, *"I want that mountain. I know that it belongs to me because God has given it to me."* Thank God! **He had the deed in his hand.** And folk, we ought to have it in our hearts or in our hands right now, because we have the promises of God. We ought to stand on them. We ought to rely on them. We ought to look at Him who is invisible, the One whom the natural eye can't see, and we ought to declare: *"God has given us the land."*

The land of your community

Right there in your community, God has given you the land. Do you know why God planted your church where He did? It was to provide your community with a witness—to shine His light into their darkness. You say, *"But it's so difficult. It's so hard."* So what! There will always be difficulties. If you wait until everything gets right, you'll never do anything. Face the problems. Face the difficulties and say, *"God has promised us that if we go, He will be with us to the end of the earth. We're standing on the promises of God, shouting the victory, and we're going to go out and take this land, this community for the glory of God."* God has given it to you. It's a matter of going out and possessing your possessions. God wants us to live in victory. There's no question about it. Jesus died for a lot more than most folk are enjoying these days.

Caleb had undiminished faith. He believed for forty-five years. He had the answer in his heart; he had a grip on the Word of God, and he was standing on the promises. That's what your church ought to be doing right now. Whenever you are faced with difficulties, problems, giants, and impossibilities, God is calling you to believe, in faith, that He is ready to do something. God will move in and do what we are unable to do. You see, Caleb said, *"We are well able because the Lord has given us the land."* We can do nothing of ourselves, but if we stand on the promises of the Word of God, nothing is impossible with Him.

No Turning Back

A word for the "half-hearted"

Caleb had wholehearted obedience. *"Trust and obey."* Caleb said. *"I wholly followed the Lord."* The reason some folk are "fainthearted" is that they are "halfhearted." That's why there are so many fainthearted people in the church. They are halfhearted. If they would be totally sold out to God, if they would embrace the promises of the Word of God so that the Word of God and the promises of God become a reality in their lives, they would be wholehearted for God. Caleb wholly followed the Lord. The people who turn back are the ones who are half-hearted and never go one hundred percent for Jesus Christ. Something happens, and they turn back. They listen to the doubters and unbelievers. They quit, rather than listen to the Word of God and to the man of God.

Be a giant-killer

Finally, we see that when there is wholehearted obedience, there is supernatural strength. There was strength to be a giant killer. Caleb said, *"I know that God has given it to me."* The rest of them died in the wilderness except for the two spies who came back with a good report. None of the others saw the land of promise. They rejected the truth when they heard it. They rejected the Word of God. They rejected the man of God. They rejected the commands of God, and as a result they could not enter into the land of promise.

After Caleb had fought battles and helped others take their land, he said, *"I want Mt. Hebron."* The biggest giants of all lived on that mountain. Think of it. He said, *"I want that mountain because it belongs to me. God gave me a deed to it 45 years ago when I spied out the land and the soles of my feet touched it. I'm going to claim what God has given me, and I'm going up that mountain. I'm going to hoist the flag. The land is mine!"*

I wonder what all God has for you that you are forfeiting

because of unbelief. I wonder what God has for your church that your church is forfeiting because you're not looking from the top-side. You're not seeing God's plan and God's purpose and God's will and God's promises. Folk, if we could embrace the promises of God, we would know that nothing is impossible for the church of the Lord Jesus Christ. **Take the land!** You have a land to take, and I pray to God that in the days to come, you will take it." **Press on. Believe God's report. The land is yours!**

24

Pressing On

A testimony—Luther Price[48]
"It has been my privilege to attend the Milldale Bible Conferences for many years. My first experience was in the mid 1970's. The floor was concrete, and the pews were planks, but the preaching and the burden for revival were wonderful. I keep going back to every conference possible because I hear sound Bible preaching that helps me grow, and I have the privilege of meeting and fellowshipping with some of God's choice men.

"Bro. Jimmy's influence and counsel have so blessed my life. Every preacher needs a pastor who is his friend, who understands his burdens and his heart to know the fullness of our God. Bro. Jimmy is that kind of person—a pastor's pastor.

"I am grateful to Milldale Baptist Church for following the vision of its pastor. Milldale's ministries, through the printed press and pulpit proclamation of the good news of Jesus Christ and His sufficiency, have circled the globe."

It's never easy for a church to transition from a long-time love and trust relationship with a pastor, to new leadership, but God faithfully shepherded Milldale Baptist Church through this period. In Bro. Jimmy's resignation letter[49], among the many he mentioned as having a special place in his heart, was Danny Greig, *"with whom I have had the privilege of serving for 25 years."* At that time, little did Danny realize that in two years he would be the pastor of Milldale Baptist Church.

---

[48] Bible teacher, HIS Ministries, Central, South Carolina
[49] See chapter one

The Milldale Story

Even as the Apostle Paul, not knowing how many days he had left, began passing the torch on to Timothy, his son in the ministry, so Bro. Jimmy, who had so faithfully carried the Milldale torch for over forty years, began signaling to others that their lap lay ahead, and that the pace he had set need not slow down, because the God he served, and serves, is their God, and Milldale's future is as bright as His promises.

The story of God's miraculous intervention in the affairs of man; the testimony of His mighty works down through history, is really "HISstory" fleshed out through His people who, surrendered to Him, become instruments in His hands to perform His purposes in their generation.

Abram was just a 75 year old businessman who had followed his father from Ur of the Chaldees to Haran until God tapped him to be the *"father of the faithful"* and called him to get up and head toward the land of promise (Genesis 12).

Moses thought he had been relegated to the Midian desert for the rest of his life until God spoke to him from a burning bush (Exodus 2).

David thought he would be shepherding and playing his harp for the rest of his life until God chose him to be a King (1 Samuel 16).

Gideon thought he'd be spending his days threshing wheat and hiding it from the Midianites until the Angel of the Lord appeared and called him a *"mighty man of valor"* (Judges 6:12).

Paul thought he would be spending his life persecuting the people who were following someone they believed to be the Messiah until his encounter with the living Christ on the Damascus road (Acts 9).

Most of the disciples thought they'd never be anything but fishermen until a man on a seashore called them to follow Him.

Then there are the scores of *ordinary people,* some known only to God, who heard "the summons," who followed, and who accomplished exploits in their generation in the name and power of the One who called.

25

Danny Greig Looks Back

"You live life going forward. You understand it looking back."
—Charles Haddon Spurgeon

Summer, 1964
"Danny, we're having a camp meeting here in Louisiana and the Lord is really moving. I want you to get on the next Greyhound bus and I'll pick you up in Baton Rouge."
"But, Dad!"
"No 'buts' about it, son. I want you to get here as quickly as possible. Do you have money for the ticket?"
"Yes, sir."

Sixteen year old Danny Greig was spending the summer with his grandparents in McAllen, Texas, while working to earn money for the next school year. His dad, Ed Greig, had recently moved the family to the city of McAllen, on the Texas-Mexican line, as it was an ideal spot to base his "bush-pilot" missionary work across the border.

As for Danny, moving to a new place was not unusual, nor was starting another grade with kids he had never met. McAllen High would be the 12th school he had attended since first grade.

But now, the phone call? Louisiana? *"Why does Dad want me to get there right away? Does this mean we're going to move again?*

Though there was a lot in life that Danny did not understand, he did know that he could trust his father, so he headed for the Greyhound bus station where he'd begin the 700 mile trip to Baton Rouge.

There was no way Danny could know what lay ahead, nor could he have begun to imagine what God had in store for his

The Milldale Story

life. He might have easily identified with C. H. Spurgeon's statement that,

"You live life going forward and you understand it looking back."

The day would come, however, when Danny would be able to clearly trace God's providential hand as it led and shaped this, sometimes reluctant, child of His.

Cajun country

His dad was waiting when he stepped off the bus in Baton Rouge. As they drove over winding country roads all his dad wanted to do was talk about what was happening at the Camp Meeting. Finally, after what seemed hours to Danny, they drove through the entrance of Milldale Baptist Church and Camp Grounds.

"I admit that I was bored up to that point, in spite of my Dad's enthusiasm," recalls Danny. "I was also still upset that I had had to give up my summer job, but as we drove on to the property I immediately sensed that something was different. And that evening I discovered why my dad was so insistent that I come.

"As the preachers preached, there was outward evidence of an inward working of the Holy Spirit in the listeners. Personal conviction was so powerful that the altar was full of people on their knees, getting right with God. The Lord began to speak softly to my heart about my becoming a preacher of the Gospel. My immediate response was, *'Not me, Lord. I can't even get through an oral book report at school, much less stand before a congregation and preach. And oh, I also know how some church members treat their pastors.'* Of course God did not respond, but the constant tug on my heart continued."

Another significant "prompting of the Lord" happened that summer at Milldale. A certain young lady caught Danny's eye, and he remembers saying flippantly, yet prophetically, to his sister, Darlene, *'I'm going to marry that girl someday.'* (July 5,

1968, Joe and Lucille Young gave Danny Greig their daughter, Nancy, in marriage.)

"As I look back on those days," recalls Danny, "I can now see more clearly the providential working of God in my life. It all began that summer of 1964, when my missionary father demanded my presence at that first Milldale Camp Meeting. *'Lord, thank you for ordering my steps!'*

"At the close of the camp meeting my family and I returned to McAllen, Texas, where I entered 10th grade. Then, when the school year ended I returned to Milldale for the summer camp meeting of 1965 where I soon discovered that my life was about to take a drastic new direction."

A new chapter

The Lord was at this time already leading Danny's parents to move to a different mission location: Mexico's Yucatan Peninsula. Since he still had two years remaining before graduating high school, and there was not an English speaking school available in Merida, Yucatan, they were faced with a dilemma—where would they send their son to school? This was when Jimmy and Frances Robertson stepped in and offered to keep Danny in their home while he finished high school.

"Looking back," recalls Danny, "I realize what a tremendous sacrifice this must have been for a young couple with three small children. But God provided the necessary grace as Bro. Jimmy and Frances became my second parents, and now, for nearly 50 years, my dearest friends.

"So it was, at summer's end in 1965, having just turned seventeen, I waved a tearful goodbye to my family and began a new chapter with the Robertsons. I was thinking then, however, that this "change of address" would be just a temporary arrangement until I finished high school, but little did I know that the Lord was preparing me for a lifelong ministry at Milldale.

26

Each Step of the Way

*"Our faithful God has promised He would lead
and guide us daily by His mighty hand.
He knows exactly what His children need
and works according to His perfect plan.
There have been mountains we've been asked to climb,
Some rivers have been wide, some skies been grey;
The valleys have been deep and dark at times,
But without fail, our God has led the way."*[50]

Life with Danny's new family began with much anxiety and insecurity. At this point he was a very shy, introverted teenager. To think of what was transpiring was frightening to him, not to mention the fact that he was intimidated by the head of this home. He went to the Lord and poured out his complaint.

"Lord, why do you always place me in the presence of deep, discerning men of God like my Dad, Manley Beasley, Sonny Holland, Jesse Norris, Curtis McCarley and now Jimmy Robertson, and expect me to be a normal person?

"It was then the Holy Spirit immediately convicted me and changed my thinking and prayer.

"Lord this is probably as difficult an adjustment for Brother Jimmy and Frances as it is for me, so please help me be a helper in this home and not a hindrance.

"From the beginning I felt accepted and loved by this godly couple. They treated me like one of their own as they have continued to do through the years.

---

[50] From the song, *Each Step of the Way*, by Ron and Patricia Owens

Always work to be done
"There was much work to be done during those early years at Milldale. Our pastor's vision may not have been immediately caught by everyone, but his Holy Spirit-led preaching and leadership was all that we needed to follow him, as he obeyed the Lord. Much like Nehemiah, the Lord used Bro. Jimmy to keep us motivated, and the Spirit gave us all *a mind to work*. On more than one occasion, I stayed home from school because my help was needed on one of the projects, and interestingly, my teachers never said a negative word because the residents in the Milldale community knew that God was up to something.

A construction-site miracle
"I remember one day when we were working on the Tabernacle roof. Bro. Collyn Richards, a giant of a man at 6'5" and 240 pounds, was walking the roof ridge when he stepped through the insulation and began falling some 36' to the ground. I watched helplessly as he fell head first toward a welding machine. Miraculously, a large extension cord began to wrap around his body and just about 6' before hitting the welding machine, the cord jerked him upright and away from the machine while partially breaking his fall. He hit the ground with a thud and then, in a split second, he was on his feet. My father-in-law, Joe Young, spontaneously ran and grabbed him. After catching his breath, he seemed to be OK. Praise God, there were no broken bones or bruises, but two weeks after this incident Collyn's hair turned completely gray! Through all these many years of work and activities, no one has ever been seriously injured on the camp grounds. *To God be the glory!*

A strange accent
"Preparations were being made for the 1965 Thanksgiving Camp Meeting, and Bro. Jimmy had informed the church that a missionary from Scotland would be one of our guest speakers. As I was returning from Zachary, after running an errand, I

noticed a small fellow walking down the shoulder of Milldale Road. He was a good distance from anywhere so I stopped and asked if he needed a ride. To my surprise he answered with an unusual accent.

"No, thank you. I am just walking and praying." That highway stranger turned out to be Dr. James Alexander Stewart. The excitement at the beginning of each camp meeting had always been overwhelming to me, but now I was even more excited with the anticipation of hearing this Scottish preacher.

God with us

"As Dr. Stewart walked to the pulpit that night I sensed something was very different about this man, and it wasn't just his strange accent or his message alone; it was the presence and power of the glory of God.

"In one particular service, as he was finishing his message and his report of revival in Europe, the Holy Spirit came like a wave of the sea. Holy Ghost conviction gripped us, and just about everyone in the building fell to his knees confessing sin, including Nancy and me. One could hear the desperate cries of brokenness and weeping all over the building. I can't remember how long this continued, but I do remember that time ceased to be an issue, and the only thing that mattered was getting to God.

"As long as the Lord grants me breath and the capacity to remember, I will never forget this glorious camp meeting. The Lord did such a deep work of revival in my own heart that I have not gotten over it to this very day. *Lord, do it again.*

School: a mission field

"The influence of revival moved into our small community and school. When I had enrolled at *Pride High School,* the closest school to Milldale, I was told that outsiders were not accepted well. I did not let this affect me as I just wanted to live for Jesus and influence the lives of those around me, but because of my shyness I felt I was the least one for God to use among these teens. That didn't keep me from praying for my fellow students, however, and soon God began His work. Several were saved and began to attend our church.[51]

"Forty-three years have passed since my high school graduation, and still, on occasion, I receive calls from former classmates who need help in one way or another. I always point them to Jesus. *"Thank you Lord for still answering my prayer."*

A testimony—Debbie Beasley
"Danny Greig was a special friend. He was like a big brother to me. He taught me how to drive and showed a lot of patience when I knocked over several garbage cans. He also was my idol. He was a great athlete and musician. As I remember, he could play just about every position on the football team, including quarterback. One year he was voted most outstanding player. He was also a very good trumpet player, so I decided to play the trumpet too!

"God used Danny as a strong witness in Pride High School. He showed that you could be a Christian and love the Lord, and also be a great athlete and musician. I don't know how many, but I do know that there were a number of students who put their faith in Jesus through Danny's witness. I thank God for the years I spent at Milldlale, and as I look back, I realize how much they had to do with what I believe, and the person I have become."

Still running
After graduating from high school, however, Danny's life became much more complicated—he was still running from God's call. He decided to enter LSU to major in agriculture and veterinarian science, as his dream was to become a veterinarian.

---

[51] God used Danny's athletic ability (he was one of *Pride High School's* outstanding football players) and his musicianship (trumpet and singing), to give him a platform from which to witness.

All entrance requirements had been completed, and thanks to his high school agriculture teacher, he had obtained a work scholarship. Everything was in place, but by the end of August the unrest had returned, and it was serious. Danny continued to pray, then at the last possible minute he made the decision to enroll at *East Texas Baptist College* (now a university).

In his father's footsteps

In the early 1950's, the mundane spiritual life of the ETBC campus had been disrupted by three young preachers who were *"sold out to Jesus"*. Their late night prayer meetings seemed to be a big part of the problem. These three men were none other than, Ed Greig, Danny's father, Manley Beasley, and Harold Brown. After his decision to attend ETBC was final, his Dad said to Danny; *"There are a couple of professors still teaching at ETBC who may remember the name Greig, so tread softly."* Danny thought: *"Thanks, Dad, for making things easier for me!"* As it turned out, not by choice, Danny ended up with the same two professors!

Uncle Sam calls

With college completed, and having been married but a few short months, the unimaginable happened—Danny received a draft notice from the U.S. Army. His heart fell into his feet. Here he was just starting life, and now it looked like it might soon end because at that moment, the Viet Nam war was at its height.

But God had special long-term plans for Danny. After boot camp at Fort Polk, Louisiana, and a three month stop-over at Fort Devens, Massachusetts, he was shipped off to South Viet Nam, 101st Airborne Division, Bien Hua Airbase.

"I remember the heartbreaking good-bye I had with all my loved ones—my church family, my Dad, Mom, sisters and brother, and my precious wife," recalls Danny. "Nancy was expecting our first child, and I seriously believed this would be the last time I would see any of them again in this life.

A Tunnel Rat?

Danny's orders instructed him to report to Special Services for two weeks of training. When he read the two words, *Special Services,* he knew that it probably meant that he would end up being a *Tunnel Rat,* because of his size. This is usually a smaller person who can fit into the tunnels made by the enemy, and their objective is to engage the enemy inside the tunnels. Life expectancy for a T*unnel Rat* at the time was three months. Danny now knew for certain that he would never see his sweetheart again.

He remembers how he wept uncontrollably that Sunday morning as he made his way to the small base chapel to be alone and pray. He began to pour out his heart to the Lord.

"Lord, please be merciful to me and let me live to serve you and see my family again."

Almost immediately the Holy Spirit reminded him of the Scripture his godly mother-in-law, Lucille Young, had written in a going-away card she had given to him. The verse was *Psalm 91:7 "A thousand shall fall at thy side, and ten thousand at thy right hand; but it shall not come nigh thee."* Peace and comfort began to flood his soul as the fear that had gripped him started to flee.

Last man standing

"After completing two weeks of training I was now part of a large formation of men standing at parade rest waiting their assignments for the next year," remembers Danny. "One by one men departed as their names were called. *'Something must be wrong,'* I thought. *I'm the last person standing in formation, and my name has not been called.'* Once again fear gripped me. *'What is happening? Tunnel Rat!' That's it. I'm headed for the tunnels.'* Then suddenly, out of the blue, a messenger from the Lord appeared in starched fatigues and spit-shined boots.

'Hey man. Are you Private Danny Greig?'
I reluctantly replied, *'Yes sir, I am.'*
'My name is Oscar Menchaca from Texas. Welcome to Special Services. Are you a Christian?'
'Yes, I am,' I joyfully exclaimed!
'Praise God! You can help me with all the heathens in our office. I've been by myself for a long time.'
'Office? Did you say office?'
'Yeah man. Thousands would like to have the job you've been assigned to.'

"Oscar and I became close friends until his departure for his home in Texas three months later. With a thankful heart to the Lord, for the following eleven months I reported to my work in a safe, clean office. My church and family back home were praying, and the Lord had answered by providing more than any of us had wisdom to ask for. **Praise His Name!**

Heading home

"The Lord, by His hand of providence, saw me through this very difficult season of life. He had protected me from harm and had comforted Nancy while I was away. I was ecstatic with excitement to see my wife again, and for the first time to hold my son Michael Edward, who was now five months old. Nancy was concerned that Michael would start crying when he saw me for the first time, but instead, he grinned as I took him into my arms. He was glad his Dad was now home! At least that is how I interpreted it."

27

Opportunities for Growth

"Being confident of this very thing, that He which hath begun a good work in you will perform it until the day of Jesus Christ"
—Philippians 1:6

"I was completely caught off guard," recalls Danny. "Bro. Jimmy was standing at the door of the church with a hymnal in his hand, and as he greeted Nancy, Michael and me, he said; *'I want you to lead the music tonight.'* He had already marked the songs that would be sung. I was not only surprised, I was scared out of my boots, but I loved him and my church too much to refuse. From that Sunday evening, for almost thirty years, I was the music director of Milldale Baptist Church.

Which way to turn?
"I had been away for what seemed to be a long time, and I had to get re-acquainted with reality and relationships. The responsibility of making a living in the midst of a recession made life even more difficult, but I gradually readjusted to civilian life, as well as to my role as husband and new father. Then, approximately two years after returning from Viet Nam, Nancy and I received the exciting news that we were expecting our second child—another boy! We named him Matthew Daniel.

"I remember being gripped with the fear of having to pay for Matthew's birth. The military had covered the cost of our first son, Michael Edward, but for this birth we had very little savings in the bank and no health insurance, so we began to put more of my meager pay check in savings, hoping to have enough to pay the final hospital and doctor bills. My prayer at

The Milldale Story

the time was, *'Dear Lord, we need your help!'*

"The annual February Camp Meeting was just days ahead when I, along with several other men, was told by our employer that we were being laid off. Laid off? What was I going to do now? How would I break this devastating news to my dear wife? I needed to pray, but I was in a backslidden condition. The Lord and I were not speaking. I felt bankrupt spiritually, and I was broke financially.

A Camp Meeting encounter

"Nancy and I agreed not to take our checkbook to any of the services because we couldn't afford to give anything. What we didn't know was that my dad had called from the mission field to ask his good friend, Bill Stafford, to *'pray for Danny, because he's not right with God.'* Bill was the guest speaker for the conference, and as the meeting began, even though the attendance that year was low, I could sense that God was going to do something.

"I confess that I really had not wanted to attend the meetings because I was running from God. As Bro. Bill preached, it was as if he were preaching to a thousand people, yet every message seemed to be directed right at me. I believe it was on Wednesday night of that week that he preached on giving. I immediately fell under conviction. As soon as the invitation was given, I made my way to the altar to repent of my backslidden heart and every known sin in my life. I felt clean again and the line of communication between God and me was restored. As soon as I finished praying, the Holy Spirit spoke to me, and it could not have been more clear than had God spoken audibly.

"'Danny, give Me your savings account.' My heart sank to my feet. *'But Lord, have you forgotten that I don't even have a job? How am I going to tell Nancy? You know what we have agreed* **not** *to do. We have a baby that is due in just three months!'*

"What I did not realize at the time was that Nancy was also at the altar experiencing the same convicting power of the Holy Spirit. We had simultaneously experienced personal revival and our deepest desire now was to be obedient to our Master. We went home and joyfully wrote a check for the full amount of our savings. Everything! We were now rich spiritually, and we were now really broke financially, at least, so we thought.

Back to earth and a test of faith

"The camp meeting ended on a high spiritual note, and we left with full hearts. The following Monday, however, I was again faced with the reality that I still had no job and no prospect of one. Nancy and I were praying desperately that the Lord would intervene. To be honest, I began to doubt. Had we made the right decision in emptying our savings account? I had heard Brother Manley preach many times that, *'after you have been obedient there will be a time of testing.'* He called this, *'the test of faith.'* I confessed my wavering condition to the Lord and prayed, *'Lord, I believe. Help Thou my unbelief!'*

Miraculous provision

"I began to submit applications anywhere and everywhere that I thought a job might be available. I was getting nowhere and was becoming more and more anxious. Then one morning, as I was turning into the parking lot of a small manufacturing company, a gentleman wearing a cowboy hat was leaving in a pickup truck. He pulled up beside me, rolled down his window and asked if he could help. I explained why I was there. He inquired about my job experience and told me that all he had available was a supervisor position. *'If you are interested,'* he said, *'come back at 3:30 this afternoon.'* Then he sped away. I returned that afternoon for an interview, and the very next morning I began working for a man who became a dear friend. My starting salary was twice as much as I had ever made in my life. I hurried home with the wonderful news!

"Three months later, on my 25th birthday, Nancy gave birth to our second child, Matthew Daniel, a beautiful baby boy. Incidentally, the hospital and doctor bills were approximately twice the amount we had estimated they would be, but because of God's abundant provision, we were able to pay cash for the full amount.

"While driving home from the hospital late that evening, June 1, 1973, I thought back over the events of the last several months. Our Lord had been so generous and faithful to Nancy and me. Though anxious about the future during that camp meeting worship service, we had simply obeyed by faith, and the Lord had blessed us. I praise God for the precious truths I have learned from our pastor, Brother Jimmy, and the other men of God who have preached at Milldale. *To God be the Glory!*"

28

God's "still small voice" Gets Louder

"God is looking for a people who'll surrender Him their all,
With their eyes fixed on the Master, ready at a moment's call
To respond to His assignment, whether short or whether long,
Willing to change their agenda to the mission God is on."[52]

A little more than a year had now passed, and though Danny was making a good salary, with bonuses and benefits, his spirit was beginning to become restless again. The silent, gentle tug of the Holy Spirit seemed to be more constant and growing stronger. He was successful as far as the world's view of success is, yet he was not happy because deep within he knew that the Lord wanted him to preach. This was frightening because he had no confidence that he could ever accomplish what God wanted him to do. There were many sleepless nights as he struggled in his heart and mind. There was no relief at church either. Brother Jimmy's messages seemed to be tailor-made for him. Finally, Danny made an appointment with him. He had to have some relief!

The answer
"Bro. Jimmy prayed with me, shared my concern, but refused to tell me what to do. I am now convinced that he was more aware of what God was doing than I realized at the time. On one occasion when I stopped in to visit the folk working in the printing ministry, Brother Jimmy asked how things were going. *'Are you still thinking about doing something else?'* he

---

[52] From the song, *God is Looking for a People*, by Ron and Patricia Owens

The Milldale Story

asked. I knew exactly what he meant. He affirmed that he was not going to make a decision for me, but he did tell me that there was a position open in the printing ministry, and if I thought the Lord was in it I could also help him with pastoral duties. *'You and Nancy pray about it and let me know.'* A few weeks later, my long tenure at Milldale began.

The print shop

"Work in the printing ministry was often hard with long hours, but always rewarding. It was so exciting to know that I literally handled Bibles and Scripture portions in foreign languages that would be sent all over the world. Another plus was having the privilege of working with Ivan Carlson. The Lord had impressed Ivan and Jackie to sell their home, resign their jobs in Florida, and move to Milldale to run the printing operation. Ivan and I spent many days and hours, sometimes all night, working on printing equipment or completing printing projects.

Times of refreshing…again

"Most of us try to forget the difficult struggles and hardships we have experienced, but I have discovered from Scripture and experience that these times are usually necessary for God to get our attention, and they're often needed to change our hearts. I do not want to give the impression that things were always rosy at Milldale. There have been storms and battles, but our Lord has always brought us through. It was in the late 1970's that our church was at a very low ebb. Attendance had fallen off drastically. Ivan, Jackie, Nancy and I were working with the youth, but there were only a few in attendance. I was also teaching a Bible class in Denham Springs, Louisiana, at the home of Ruth and Bill Cook, Brother Jimmy's sister and brother-in-law. Their large den would be packed with youth each time we met.

"The Holy Spirit began to stir our hearts to pray and seek the Lord. We experienced a touch of revival. Among the young people in attendance were two brothers, James and Mike Courtney, who had recently been saved. God had not only saved these two young men, but had also called them to preach the Gospel, and to this day they have not only been faithful servants of the Lord, but they have also been my dear friends.

A touch of revival
"The news spread quickly that the Lord was once again doing a wonderful work at Milldale. Teens began to drive in from surrounding communities and towns, and soon there were more youth than adults. Many would show up on Saturdays to hand out tracts and witness. These teens were on fire for the Lord. They loved to sing, so we started a choir. It was not long before our church bought a bus, and we traveled to many churches in the area on Sunday evenings. The youth choir would sing and testify, and then I would preach. These were *times of refreshing from the presence of the Lord!*

The church
"Milldale Baptist Church itself began to experience rapid growth. Like-minded people started to join our church family—people who desired to hear good Biblical preaching, and who had a heart for missions and a love for the camp meetings. It was soon necessary to remodel the large tabernacle to handle the influx of new members, and Brother Jimmy felt that it was necessary, at this point, for me to be his full-time assistant pastor. Although I continued to be closely involved with the printing ministry, my days of physical labor in the print shop ended.

"As the years rolled on the Lord continued to bless the church and the Camp Meeting ministry until the day arrived that I had often dreaded—Brother Jimmy broke the news to me that he was retiring from the pastorate. I had been honored and blessed to have served under his leadership for 27 years. He had been my mentor, confidante, and friend. He had protected me and had stood with me even in those times when I was wrong. His family had sacrificed on many occasions so that my family would be taken care of financially. He had overlooked my faults and encouraged me to go forward. He and Frances, then and now, have continually prayed for us and loved us like their own. This Godly couple are my and Nancy's heroes in the faith. Frances is a Christian model for every pastor's wife. I have never known her to speak her opinion in a public service, but she quietly and reverently relays her opinion to her husband.

"Brother Jimmy's retirement was not imminent—he didn't actually retire until three years later—so I did have time to decide whether I wanted to become a candidate for senior pastor. After much contemplation and prayer, I finally came to the painful conclusion that it would be best for the church if I declined. What the church needed, I reasoned, was a complete new staff, so it was with mixed emotions that I explained to Bro. Jimmy that I was resigning to begin an itinerate ministry."

A brief change

In October, 2001, Danny and Nancy launched into their new travelling ministry, and after almost a year of praying and searching, they became members of New Bethlehem Baptist Church in Watson, Louisiana, where their dear friend, James 'Bubba' Courtney, was, and is, the pastor. When Danny was not away in a meeting, he ministered in music and sometimes preached at the church. They fell in love with the saints of New Bethlehem, as this dear church family ministered to them. Then, after two years on the road, they sensed they were to return to Milldale.

A growing hunger

"During the period we had been away," Danny recalls, "I had been involved in a systematic study of the history of revival. My heart was hungering for God to, 'do it again.' Nancy and I began to pray about rejoining the church, and it was a joyful Sunday morning when we once again became members of the family of God at Milldale.

"Though it seemed a little strange to be joining the church that we had been a part of for so many years, the truth is, our hearts had never left the people and place where God had moved so deeply in the past. We were glad to be back! This gave Brother Jimmy and me the opportunity to again spend time together. I had missed his close friendship, though on occasions, I had been able to drive him to meetings. It was so good to hear him preach again. Fellowship with all of our old friends was renewed, and it seemed as if we had never left. Everyone made us feel welcome.

"Then, in January, 2006, the unexpected happened. Brother Gary DarDar, who had become Milldale's pastor when Bro. Jimmy retired in 2004, resigned, and I was asked to be the interim pastor.

God's call evolves

"As is often the case, several families left the church when Brother Gary resigned, and as I looked at the situation, the task seemed daunting. This time, however, I knew the Lord was leading me to be a part of reviving the work that He had started.

"I confess to feeling intimidated as I thought of pastoring Brother Jimmy and Brother Sonny, but both these men, with over 100 years of faithful preaching and ministry between them, prayed for me and encouraged me. And I surely needed their prayers! In less than three months, the church had called me as full-time senior pastor.

"I knew this would be the greatest challenge of my life and ministry because many believed that Milldale's glory days were past. I was told that we would never again experience the presence and power of God that we had once known. But, in spite of these negative reports, I took a step of faith, trusting

The Milldale Story

God to do what so many felt was impossible. I accepted the church's call to be their pastor."

A testimony—Bill Sturm[53]

"When Milldale Baptist Church called Brother Danny Greig as its pastor, they did a good thing. He understands and has a love for this ministry and its workings. I know God has many great things in the future for him and for this church which has been the foundation of all the Milldale ministries."

Prepared for God's assignment

This call to be pastor of Milldale Baptist Church was the culmination of many years of preparation. Danny had sat at the feet of some of God's greatest servants. He had been exposed to the teachings of men of faith such as his father, Ed Greig, Ron Dunn, Bill Stafford, Jesse Norris, Harold Brown, Manley Beasley, and of course his closest friends, Jimmy Robertson and Sonny Holland. He had heard of the mighty movings of God in revival from the lips of James Alexander Stewart, Oswald J. Smith, C. L. Culpepper, Miss Bertha Smith and Duncan Campbell. He had experienced those moments at Milldale when heaven had touched earth and glory filled the land, He had observed miracle after miracle take place on those 16 acres as lives were transformed. He had witnessed God's miraculous provision as Milldale's leaders stepped out on faith to believe Him for the impossible.

God's work

"My greatest desire was, and still is, to see God once again visit us with, as the old-timers used to put it, *'Holy Ghost revival.'* I spent much time on my knees," Danny remembers, "seeking God for wisdom and direction. I must confess that there were times I would get discouraged and wanted to give

---

[53] Bill Sturm, evangelist, Valdosta, Georgia

up. Midst those times of agony of soul, the Lord blessed me with personal revival. My encounters with Holy God in the past at Milldale, and my study of revivals in history so moved and changed me that I began feeling as though I were living under an open heaven.

"One of my requests of the Lord was that He make me a man of prayer. I was convinced that the only way we would see the longing of our hearts fulfilled was through faith and prayer. Brother Jimmy had taught us that principle, and we had seen from first-hand experience that this was the only way to see God work supernaturally. I was driven to my knees, and I remember praying, *'Lord this is Your ministry, this is Your work. It's way too big for me, so I turn it all over to You. Whatever it takes.'*

"This simple prayer of surrender brought great relief. The Lord soon began doing a supernatural work within me and our congregation, though it did not happen as I had envisioned. I confess that deep within my motives, what I really wanted was for God to make things easier for me and cause the ministry to go smoothly. God, however, did not choose to answer my prayer that way. His plan would not have been one of own choosing."

29

Through Tragedy to Victory

"Therefore, do not lose heart...for the momentary light affliction is producing for us an eternal weight of glory, far beyond all comparison. While we look not at the things which are seen but at the things that are not seen, for the things that are seen are temporal, but the things that are not seen are eternal."
(2 Corinthians 4:16-18 NASB)

"Someday, I'll see the reason for it all.
Someday, all my heartaches and questions will seem so small.
Someday joy will break through sadness,
Someday grief will turn to gladness,
Someday, when I see my Lord—
'Till that 'someday' I'll trust Him with it all."[54]

Danny shares

"In February, 2006, a longtime member of our church and devoted intercessor, Lena Partin, entered the hospital for surgery. She was well up in years, but strong and healthy. Following the operation she had a stroke and went to be with her Lord. I miss the prayer meetings we often had in her home.

"In May of that same year, the Lord reached down and took Eddie Duncan from us. He and his family had been a part of Milldale since he was a teenager. He was only 54. I was beginning to see that our Lord was using grief to bind our church family together in cords of love and grace. Then, while praying for strength in the midst of our hurting hearts, the unfathomable happened.

---

[54] From the song, *Someday*, by Patricia Owens

Why?

"One short month after Eddie's death, and only two days into our summer Teen Retreat, we received the shocking and totally unexpected news of our oldest son's death. June 20, 2006, will forever be etched in our minds. My family, and our church family were devastated beyond measure. The Apostle Paul so aptly described our state of being with these words, *"We were pressed out of measure, above strength, insomuch that we despaired even of life"* (1 Cor. 1:8).

"After an autopsy, it was determined that Michael had died from a dissecting aorta aneurysm. We know, however, and believe it was God's will to take our son at this time. I had preached that life and death are in the hands of our sovereign Lord, and that we do not believe in accidents, but trust in His providence. It was much easier for me to preach these truths, but now I was finding it much more difficult to trust God's wisdom during this time of deep grief. I found myself asking God, **"Why?"**

"**Why** our son? He was only 36 years old. **Why** our son? He had a wonderful Christian wife and four beautiful children whom he loved dearly. Michael had recently received his captain's bars as a pilot and instructor. His dream was at last being fulfilled. He had a great love for flying, just like his missionary grandfather, Ed Greig. Also, and most importantly, we could all see him growing deeper in his relationship with his Lord. Almost on a daily basis, I continued to ask the Lord, '*Why?*'

"I had a profound sense of inadequacy to continue pastoring the church, and for as long as a year, I contemplated resigning. As anyone who has experienced the loss of a loved one knows, I found it very difficult to stay focused mentally. I was depleted physically and emotionally and often cried to the Lord, '*How can I effectively minister to others while I am in this condition?'*

The Milldale Story

What now?

"My dear wife, Nancy, and I were reading books and articles on coping with loss and grief, and most were helpful. However, as I was re-reading *When Heaven Is Silent,* by my longtime friend and mentor, Ron Dunn, he made a profound statement that helped me immensely. He explained that **"Why?"** is the wrong question to be asking. The more important question is **"What now?"** The Holy Spirit shined light and strength into my hurting soul, and now I was willing and able to move forward. Thank you, Brother Ron. Although you are presently in heaven, you continue to minister to us.

"We received the news of Michael's passing on Tuesday morning, and almost immediately our loving church family and community began arriving at our home. They just loved us and took care of us during this awful time. My family experienced what Christianity is all about. Brother Jimmy and Frances were by our side constantly helping and praying for us. Not just for the moment, but for at least a year, Brother Jimmy would call every day to check on us. Brother Sonny and Dorothy would often stop by our home just to let us know that they loved us and were praying for us. We could not have made it if it had not been for our church family at Milldale.

"In retrospect, I see more clearly what God was doing during this time. He was certainly working in our hearts, but also, through our deep trials, He was uniting our church by a deepening love for one another and to a greater dependence on our Lord.

"This spirit has continued, and now, once again, we are becoming keenly aware of the presence of the Holy Spirit in our worship services. Souls are being saved and the Lord is adding to our church family. ***To God be the glory!***

The future

"My vision for the future of this ministry is to continue what God started many years ago in the heart of a young preacher who had a deep longing to experience the working of a supernatural God in revival—a young man who refused to be satisfied with mediocrity and the status quo of modern day religion. He was a daring man of prayer and faith, one who believed that anything is possible if God initiates it. He was a man with a heart for world-wide missions and evangelism. He envisioned a place where discouraged, despondent pastors, evangelists, missionaries and laymen could come and hear fiery, Spirit-anointed preaching, have fellowship with other saints of God, and leave stirred and revived.

"This humble man who repels accolades and limelight, and prefers others before himself, has been my pastor, friend, and second dad. In the midst of the gargantuan day-to-day responsibilities of a pastor, camp leader, and director of *Milldale International Ministries,* he took the time to pour himself into an unlikely young man. It has been my enormous privilege and honor to have served under the leadership of my brother in Christ, Jimmy Robertson. He, and the precious Holy Spirit, have passed on to me the vision of God's ministry here at Milldale. I look to the Lord for strength and wisdom to carry this vision on for Him.

"On the back wall of the tabernacle at Milldale is a Scripture promise that I have claimed as my own. ***Faithful is he that calleth you, who also will do it** (1 Thess. 5:24 KJV).* ***Amen! So be it, Lord!***

Epilogue

As exciting as the past has been, with its ups and downs, *The Milldale Story* is not only an account of history, it is the on-going story of God's activity in our day. As the ministry presses on, the prayer is not only, *"Lord, do it again,"* but, *"Lord, accomplish through us, today, Your purposes for this hour."*

The branches of the Milldale Tree are alive and well. God continues to use the Camp Meeting and Conference ministry to radically change lives and encourage the saints, as His Word is powerfully proclaimed by Spirit-anointed preachers. "Behind the scenes," family, church members and volunteers still provide the personnel to keep the grounds, food, and lodging wheels turning.

Every summer, during the **Milldale Teen Camps,** hundreds of young people are challenged with the claims of a risen Savior; drawing them to saving faith and calling them into His service.

The **Literature Ministry**, through the *Fires of Revival* paper, continues to be a source of inspiration, challenge, encouragement and blessing to thousands of readers at home and abroad. Added, in recent years, are the ***Fires of Revival* Conferences** held in churches across the land.

International Missions remains on the front burner of Milldale Baptist Church. Through this body of believers, not only are ministries and missionaries prayed for and financially supported, but teams are regularly sent out to other nations, such as Nicaragua, one of the countries where Evangelist Sonny Holland has an extensive ministry.

If you have never "experienced" Milldale, you might consider making your way to East Baton Rouge Parish and the place where, over the years, thousands have encountered the living God; a place described by one as *"a battery charger,"* and by another as, *"a land flowing with milk and honey."*

Appendix One

Milldale Wives

Houses and wealth are inherited from fathers, but a prudent wife is from the Lord" (Proverbs 19:14).

You've seen her sitting beside her husband. You've watched her leave with her children before an extra long service has ended so she can get them to bed and ready for the next school day. Through the years you would find her back in the conference kitchen helping prepare meals for the guests, or washing dishes, or cleaning rooms and making up beds. She has kept the home-fires burning while her husband has been out on the road ministering. She is a Milldale wife.

Though there are many who could give testimony to what goes on "behind the scenes," none has been closer to the action, from the beginning, than Bro. Jimmy's wife, Frances, the "First Lady" of The Milldale Story.

Frances Robertson

"I appreciate, and am humbled by the term, "First Lady," though I've always considered myself just one of the group. From the very beginning instead of pomp and glory, there was simply lots of hard work to be done. In those early days, the church and the camp were interwoven. The main ministry of the church was the camp meetings. While the men took care of all the construction and the outside work, we ladies took charge of most of the inside jobs. During the first four or five years the Camp provided sheets, pillow slips, and blankets for all the guests. Back then we made up every single bed beforehand, and we washed all of the linens afterwards. We cleaned and painted rooms, cooked meals, washed dishes and anything else that

The Milldale Story

needed to be done. Later, we also helped with the printing, addressing, and mailing of *Fires Of Revival,* on a monthly basis.

Fun times

"I remember once when Jimmy's sister, Geraldine, and Ocia Collier, put red beans on to soak in preparation to feed a camp-meeting crowd. They didn't know how much they were going to need to prepare so they put plenty of beans on to soak. The next morning they had swelled and covered the table and kitchen floor. They considered burying them so no one would know about the mistake, but Geraldine said, *'No, we can't do that. They will eventually sprout and Jimmy will know what we did!'* They decided to cook what they needed for the camp and throw the rest away. Of course, Jimmy Robertson found out about it anyway. We still laugh about all those beans.

Before there were dishwashers there were dish-washers!

"At that time we used all glass dishes, and we had no commercial dishwasher. Everything had to be washed by hand for each meal, but the people joyfully worked. Some of the ladies washed dishes from the end of one meal to the beginning of the next. Many times I barely got home in time to change for the evening services. We may not have had time to have "ladies meetings" per se, but we would have revival among ourselves while we worked.

Breakfast

"For quite a few years we prepared a big breakfast of eggs, sausage and biscuits, served family style. Finally, the breakfast menu evolved into cereal, milk and fresh fruit. Brian Keiser, a young man on disability income, began providing fresh apples, oranges, grapefruit, and bananas for each conference, and he continues to do so to this day.

"Brian shares his testimony: *'Milldale Baptist Conference has helped me learn to order a lot of tracts and booklets to witness with, thanks to Brother Clinton Lee. And I love to continue providing produce (fruit) for the Bible Conferences. Thanks be to God for Milldale.'*

"We usually kept a house-full of preachers in our home, and they always enjoyed staying up half the night fellowshipping with one another. Our children slept wherever they could—usually in our living room on the couch or the floor in order to allow our guests to have their rooms. On one occasion, when all the preachers were sitting around in the living room talking, one of them asked James, our youngest son, why he hadn't gone to bed. James replied, *"I can't. You're sitting on it!"*

Dr. and Mrs. James Stewart stayed with us. Having been an outstanding soccer player as a youth, he could put a ball on the ground and kick it into a basketball goal. He amazed the kids once by kicking a soccer ball over the roof of the huge tabernacle. The young people would often gather at our home and play basketball with him.

"Manley Beasley, Curtis McCarley, Sonny Holland, Hyman Appleman, Leonard Ravenhill were also among the many we hosted in our home, as were Ron and Kaye Dunn who became special friends and part of the family. What special memories, filled with the sense that we were participating in something 'out-of-the-ordinary,' something that really is difficult to explain, something that God was doing.

Dorothy Holland
(Mrs. Sonny Holland)

Florida bound

"As I look back on almost 50 years of ministry, I can see how God has been there through it all. We left our partnership in *Holland Brothers Contractors,* sold our new dream home, and left our pastor, Jimmy Robertson, and our friends at Bluff Creek Baptist Church behind, to go and pastor Fairlawn Baptist

The Milldale Story

Church in Ft. Pierce, Florida. At the time, we had no idea what God's plan was going to be four years later; all Sonny knew was that he had been called to be an evangelist, but that first, God would train him as a pastor so he could better minister to His church.

Adjusting to a new role

I had not realized how different the life of a pastor's wife would be. I loved the dear Fairlawn people, and I loved Jesus, but I also loved my husband and children, and now it seemed that the circle of our family had widened, and there was a church full of folk who wanted Sonny's time as much as we did. I had left everything to follow God's call and did not look at it as a sacrifice, but I soon discovered that God was going to use those next few years to show me I was not as surrendered as I thought I was. Through many experiences and tears, God was preparing me and my children to share Sonny with the whole world.

Back to Louisiana

"Milldale was still in its infancy when we returned four years later. All that we owned was in a U-Haul trailer and when we arrived we had no place to put our belongings and we had no money. Yet, as I look back, we were not afraid, though we did have to face the reality that we needed to find a place to live.

Brother Jimmy and Frances took us and our three children into their home without knowing how long it was going to be. In a few weeks, however, Sonny did find an old house that was full of hay, and after they had cleaned out the hay, they took me to see it. I cried. Those were days of adventure! The first time I took a shower I had the company of a rat the size of a rabbit.

"We knew by faith that this would not be permanent. Sonny's brother had built a small spec house across the road from Milldale, next door to Bro. Jesse and Muriel Norris' home. As it was being finished, Curtis McCarley, who was at Milldale in a revival, said he'd be willing to buy the house and rent it to us for the note. God spoke to my heart that since the rent would be the same as the note, why shouldn't we buy it ourselves?

A mortgage miracle

"So off I went to see the insurance company that had financed our 'dream home' before we went to Florida. I remember sitting in his office and telling him our story and how we needed a loan. The agent asked about our finances, and I remember saying, *'No, Sonny doesn't have a job. We're in the hands of God, living by faith, and He will take care of it. No, we don't have a down payment.'* He looked at me and laughed. *'You want me to finance this house, and you don't know where the first month's payment will come from?'* I said, *'Oh, no, Mr. Carter, I know. It will come from God'*

"As he listened I saw tears in his eyes. He approved the loan and said if I had any problem paying a note to let him know. Incidentally, we never did need his help! We took the $500 that was left over above the cost of the house loan and bought "our evangelist" two new suits and a suitcase. Praise God, we were ready for evangelism!

A special kind of manna

"Jimmy's brother had a hog farm in Tickfaw, and he had a contract with a bread company that allowed him to pick up all their expired bread, cakes and cookies, to feed his hogs. He would send us word when he had a load, and we would go and climb into the back of that truck. It was so exciting! It was like we had found treasure. We would get enough to last our families for weeks. Bro. Jimmy had given us an old freezer, and most of the time it was full of that hog food, but we surely did enjoy it!

The church

"Milldale Church and Camp became our life. We worked, prayed, and rejoiced together as God met our daily needs. And we wept together as well, as the trials came, but the payoff was the glory of God in our midst.

"As Frances Robertson has said, we ladies did not have much time for fellowship apart from meeting at the church. With being wives, moms to our children, and encouragers to our neighbors in times of need, we had little time left. We were following a vision; we had a mission, and there was work to do. We did find, however, real enjoyment in our labors together. Through the years, folks have been amazed and delighted to see the unity and love we had and still have for each other.

Camp meetings

"We always looked forward to the Camp Meetings. These meetings went from Monday through Friday, all day long, and sometimes they even lasted all night as the men would stay and pray while we ladies went home to get the children to bed and ready for school the next day.

"When I think of all the miracles that took place in our lives, the only way I can explain it is that we worshiped and praised God, believed, and obeyed Him. Our children grew up in this atmosphere of revival, sacrifice and faith, and oh, yes, repentance, because we were not without fault. We were not without our personal sins and failures, but we always found forgiveness and cleansing as God would restore us back into fellowship with Himself. Our children also learned, along with us, that our God is real and is an ever present help in times of trouble.

"Some had a harder time than others coping with life's temptations, but as has been said, there are many, right now, scattered around the world, serving God. And we are now seeing second and third generations of young men and women attending Milldale Camps today.

Appendix One: Milldale Wives

"Our greatest joy is to see those who have been touched by the ministry of Milldale standing firm on the solid rock foundation they experienced through the years. We have watched as God has brought so many of them through the fire, and we have watched God use that fire to temper them into faithful servants of His.

Nancy Greig
(Mrs. Danny Greig)

"I have had the privilege of being a member of Milldale Baptist Church since its inception in the summer of 1963. I was 12 ½ years old (at that age the ½ is important) and a brand new Christian with no idea of the journey of faith I was about to embark upon.

"Approximately one year earlier my parents informed my sisters and me that we would be leaving the only church I'd ever known, Plank Road Baptist, and that we would start attending Bluff Creek Baptist. Our friends, Brother Sonny and Dorothy Holland, had told us about their young pastor who was on fire for the Lord. I was not very happy about changing churches as I did not want to leave my friends, but thank God for parents who followed the leadership of the Holy Spirit, regardless of my whining!

"The Lord quickly knit my family's heart together with the heart of Brother Jimmy Robertson and his dear family. We lived approximately 15 miles from the church, so they often would graciously invite us to come to the parsonage for Sunday lunch. This was the beginning of a lifelong friendship.

"During our time at Bluff Creek Baptist Church I not only sat under the soul-stirring, convicting preaching of my pastor, but was also exposed to other anointed evangelist/preachers such as Jesse Norris and Manley Beasley, as well as a feisty and fiery missionary pilot/preacher named Ed Greig. Only God knew at the time that he would one day be my father-in-law.

It was during this period that the Lord began making me aware of my lost condition. I had been in church all of my 12 ½ years. I had participated in all the activities the church offered, and I'm eternally grateful to my godly parents, Joe and Lucille Young, who gave me a wonderful foundation in God's Word during those early formative years.

Conviction

"In May of 1963, just prior to Brother Jimmy's leaving Bluff Creek Baptist to start the church and camp ministry in the Milldale community, he had Evangelist Manley Beasley come for a week of "revival services." I had already been under conviction, and as I listened to Bro. Manley, it seemed as if his eyes penetrated right through my sinful heart, exposing and revealing my desperate need of the Savior.

Friday night, as the invitation was given, I immediately responded, and Brother Jimmy graciously talked to me and prayed with me as I asked for forgiveness and submitted my life to the Lord. The following night Brother Manley spoke to the teens and preteens, encouraging and admonishing us to begin praying that the Lord would give us wisdom in all matters of our lives, but especially in choosing a spouse.

Praying for a husband

"Having just been saved, and eager to seek God's will for my life, I did begin to pray that the Lord would one day provide a godly husband for me, but I never dreamed He would bring him into my life as soon as He did. By God's providence, and I believe in answer to my simple prayer of faith, the very next year, the summer of 1964, a 16 year old young man would reluctantly attend the first camp meeting that was held in a tent on the grounds of the newly formed Milldale Baptist Church. This young man would one day become my husband. Years later, as I related this story to Mrs. Ruth Stewart, wife of Dr.

James A. Stewart, she said in her sweet soft voice and with smiling eyes, *'It didn't take Him long to answer you, did it?'*

"My mother was evidently impressed with him and commented on what a nice and considerate young man Danny Greig was. She evidently had her eye on him before I did. By August, Dan and I began a courtship that led to our marriage three years later, in July of 1968.

A spiritual high
"The year 1965 will always be a memorable year in my life, not only because it marked the beginning of our courtship, but also because it was a time when we experienced a powerful move of God in our midst. I remember it well.

"One evening as the service came to a close, there was such a holy atmosphere that permeated the tabernacle, it seemed as if one could literally hear a rushing wind in our midst as we fell on our faces before the Lord. We had become so conscious of our sinfulness, while at the same time we were sensing God's unfathomable grace and mercy! Being a teenager and such a young Christian at the time, I remember being somewhat frightened, yet in awe of God's holy presence.

"No one seemed to want to leave for fear of quenching the Holy Spirit, but eventually, as people began to disperse, I remember Brother Sonny Holland gathering some of the youth together outside on the grounds to have a time of prayer before going home. As we formed a circle and held hands, he asked each of us how God had spoken to us that night, and he encouraged us to seek God's will for our lives. Once again the Holy Spirit took over and this gracious work of God that I experienced in my early years left an indelible mark on my life. It affected not only my home life, but also my school life where some of my Christian friends and I would gather at recess and pray for one another. We would pray that we would stay strong in the Lord and be a witness among our classmates.

The Milldale Story

A military bride

"In 1969 Dan and I had been married about a year when he was drafted. I had moved to Massachusetts to be with him, thinking he would be stationed there for awhile, but our plans were turned upside down—he received orders for South Viet Nam.

"My heart was so heavy at the prospect of being apart from my dear husband for a year, especially having just received confirmation that our first child was on his way. As we drove back down to Louisiana for Danny to say goodbye to family and friends, we were experiencing conflicting emotions—being thrilled that we were on our way home, yet frightened and uneasy about Danny's going into a war zone. We were ecstatic about becoming parents for the first time, yet extremely saddened and disappointed that Danny would not be with me for the birth of our first child.

"As we drove up the driveway of my parent's home, I noticed that there were no cars under the carport. I thought to myself, *'Didn't they know we were coming home?'* But then, remembering the reports of how God was working, we decided to drive over to the church to see if anyone was there. Sure enough, there were cars everywhere, and as we got out of our vehicle we could hear singing coming from the little prayer chapel on the front of the church property.

Immediately, exhaustion turned into exhilaration and excitement as we opened the doors to the chapel and saw our family and friends joyfully worshiping and praising the Lord in song and testimony. When everyone realized that we had walked in, there was more rejoicing over our safe return home as well as praying that God would continue to protect Danny and bring him safely back from Viet Nam. God graciously and abundantly answered our prayers, for by the end of September 1970 Danny had returned home, not only to me, but also to his five month old son Michael Edward. What a joyful day!

Appendix One: Milldale Wives

Milldale life

"I have fond memories of cleaning dormitories, making up beds, working in the kitchen and dining hall, helping watch the little children while their moms and dads worked, as well as running errands when I could drive. I remember hearing Frances, our pastor's wife, along with other ladies, laughing and singing to the Lord as they prepared meals for the conferences and during times of construction.

Godly influences

"I recall a precious sister, Ocia Collier, who worked tirelessly in the early days of the ministry and is still a member of our congregation today. There were also other godly ladies who were used of the Lord to impact my life. Mrs. Jesse Norris, one of my Sunday School teachers, and Marthé Beasley, Brother Manley's wife who showed me how to have fun in the Lord. Then there were Miss Bertha Smith, Mrs. Ruth Stewart Fajfr, and Mrs. Pam Hession who all displayed devout commitment to the Lord's work and to their husbands. There was also Mrs. Kaye Dunn-Robinson, then wife of evangelist Ron Dunn, who by their example helped Dan and me survive the unexpected death of our son. Then there is my dear friend, Jackie Carlson, who has consistently shown me what real joy looks like.

"I've kept a final tribute for my mother-in-law, Janell Greig, the wife of that feisty and fiery missionary pilot/preacher who has been mentioned earlier. Through the years I have watched her go from "pillar to post," sometimes at a moment's notice when her husband told her that God said it was time to move. She followed! I watched her sacrificial willingness to *lay down her Isaac,* my Dan, leaving him with another family, in a little country community named Milldale, in order to go with her husband and other four children to the mission field. Her submissive attitude toward the Lord and her husband played a role in God's answering a twelve-year-old young girl's prayer for a godly husband.

"How quickly the years have passed. I find myself, through God's providence, still a member of Milldale Baptist Church, though no longer a 12 ½ year old but now the pastor's wife. I still find it hard to believe. I've such wonderful, godly role models, such as Frances Robertson, whose shoes I will never be able to fill!

"Now, as I think of my longtime pastor, Brother Jimmy, and my faithful husband, Danny, my thoughts go to the apostle Paul and the relationship he had with young Timothy through the years as he exhorted him, and sometimes reprimanded him (1 & 2 Timothy). Then in Philippians 2: 19-23, Paul highly commended Timothy to the Christians at Philippi. In verse 22 he says, *"...you know his proven character, that as a son with his father he served with me in the gospel."* And in Philippians 3: 17 Paul exhorted the brethren to *"... join in following my example...as you have us for a pattern."*

"Finally, I want to again personally thank Brother Jimmy and Frances for being that example and pattern that we can confidently follow as we continue to carry the torch. Our prayer is, as the song says, *"May all who come behind us find us faithful."*

Muriel Norris[55]
(Mrs. Jesse Norris)

"Though there were major family adjustments to be made when we moved from Pineville, Louisiana, to join Bro. Jimmy Robertson in the establishing of the Milldale ministry, we immediately felt a part of that 'little flock,' as my dear husband used to call us. From the beginning we understood that there was a race to be run and a race we wanted to run well. Under

---

[55] An earlier part of Muriel Norris' testimony is included in Chapter 7

the leadership of dear Pastor Jimmy Robertson, we were informed of that race, and we were warned of the devil's attempt to sidetrack us.

"I felt we were in the warmest of fellowships where there was always a petition for guidance and direction. Prayers were offered for each other, and there was always a cry for our own children.

"There were times God called us to give of our best to the Master, to give of our money as well as our time. The group at Milldale always had to depend on God. We knew that if He did not provide, the needs would not be met. There was food to buy, extra utilities to pay, cooks to help with the food preparations, and we always needed more dormitory rooms.

"At one meeting, Bro. Jimmy asked that we give a special offering to meet these expenses. The Lord gave me a number which I quietly wrote on the flyleaf of my Bible. I was really excited when Jesse came in to tell me the Lord had given him the same exact amount. And that is true when the Lord asks something of you, *'He is faithful to supply it.'* How often He asks us to exercise our faith! I remember reading somewhere that it's only here on earth that we are required to exercise faith, and how important this is, because the exercise of faith keeps us from becoming weak and ineffective.

"The subject of faith is the one thing God calls to mind and challenges my heart with more than any other subject. Oh, to be counted a faithful child of God! Milldale camp grounds and conference center presented a call to faithfulness. And there were many other areas of the Christian walk in which we had the opportunity to grow. Though at this point in life I find it difficult to remember details, suffice it to say that my life has been greatly enriched by having lived at Milldale. I have been taught by the best of preachers under the direction of the Holy Spirit.

"When we moved back to Pineville in 1974, I took with me the secret of the Christian life, God's Holy Word, and a wealth of experiences and memories. These experiences and memories are written on the blackboard of my heart. These help me find strength for today and hope for tomorrow at the dawning of every new day. My dear husband, Evangelist Jesse Norris, went to be with the Lord on October 22, 2005. He had asked Bro. Jimmy to conduct his funeral service,[56] and Milldale again came to our aid, helping us through this crisis in our life! How sweet is the Spirit of the Living God.

"I always wanted to pass on the spirit of Milldale, what it stands for, to its children and its children's children. Though some went on to have their waltz with the world after their graduation from high school, many have returned to the God of their childhood and are now serving in churches all over the world. I know that they can never forget what they have seen and heard. We pray that many others who are still outside will wake up. I believe they will, because the work God started in them will one day be completed.

"God bless the many that are ministering at Milldale today, and may He abundantly reward them for their faithfulness in the work of Revival!"

Marthé Beasley
(Mrs. Manley Beasley)

"When we first moved to Milldale from Myrtle, Mississippi, we lived in a trailer. Six in a trailer was quite an experience. We then rented a house for awhile before building our own. I had always wanted to live in a gingerbread house and so that is what we built. I had one stipulation, however, and I made this clear with Mr. Valentine, our builder—since we would be on a septic tank system, I wanted to make sure that the commodes would never back up! Downstairs or upstairs—no backing-up toilets! He promised me that he could do that, but in

---

[56] See chapter 21 for Jimmy Robertson's tribute to his friend Jesse Norris

order to guarantee I'd never have a problem he was going to have to set the tank extra deep in the ground.

"He assigned the hole digging to a teenager who was working for him. That teenager's name was Danny Greig. Danny told us later that he dug and he dug and he dug, and by the time he had finished digging that hole, the house was almost built.

"The six years we lived at Milldale were very special. There was always something going on. And oh, the camp meetings. What glorious days! People came from everywhere. Then, between the conferences, things didn't seem to slow down that much. The printing of Bibles and other biblical literature never stopped. Then there was the shipping part of the ministry and, of course, the on-going church activities.

"After six years Manley decided that we needed to move west. We didn't understand all the reasons why but we knew that part of it had to do with what was happening in the schools. There was just a lot of tension. He had wanted to move to Texas, but nothing opened up in the Lone-Star State, so we ended up with a small farm near the Louisiana-Texas line. The move was providential because it was not long before Manley began getting sick and would soon end up in Intensive care for six months in a Houston hospital.

"Though we no longer lived at Milldale, Milldale never stopped living in us. Bro. Jimmy and Frances and the rest of the Milldale family remained our closest friends. Manley enjoyed returning there more than anywhere else; in fact, he went back to be with his "Milldale friends" just a few weeks before he died."

Appendix Two

In Their Own Words[57]

Clinton and Viola Lee[58]

"I was a policeman with the Baton Rouge Police Department in 1978 when Viola and I began hearing about the printing ministry at Milldale. We heard that they were printing in fourteen different languages, and this mission outreach really stirred me to want to get involved. We were living in Baker, Louisiana, at the time, not far from Milldale and decided that the Lord would have us join our lives with this ministry and help as much as we could, even while I continued my job in law enforcement.

Called to serve Milldale's seniors

"In December, 1983, Jimmy Robertson asked me if I was eligible to retire from the police department. He wanted my wife and me to join the staff at Milldale as Senior Adult Leaders and teachers for the Senior Adult Sunday School Class. After checking with the police department's retirement system, I found that I had twenty-seven actual years of police department service, plus three years in the military, so I could actually retire with thirty years of service. After a week or two of prayer about the matter, I told Bro. Jimmy that I would retire and join the Milldale staff.

"I wrote a letter to the Chief of Police and told him that God had opened another door of ministry for me, and it was my decision to walk through it. Chief Pat Bonanno said, *'I don't know what you are talking about, but I guess it's all right. But*

---

[57] See complete list of testimonies on page 253.
[58] Clinton Lee has served Milldale Baptist Church as Senior Adult and Missions pastor for many years.

Appendix Two: In Their Own Words

wait! You're on the promotional list for the rank of Major! Are you going to pass this up?' I said, *'The decision has been made. I will retire March 1, 1984.'* I then began to serve as the Senior Adult Minister at Milldale.

More study
"With Bro. Jimmy's blessing, I took a sabbatical to study at what is now Columbia International University, and in June, 1988, I received my Certificate in Biblical Studies. Viola and I then returned to Louisiana where I directed the *Baton Rouge Seaman's Center* for a year before returning to Milldale to resume leadership of the Senior Adult work.

"Our seniors have a heart for missions and have always given generously to our class mission outreach each month. We have had great support from our pastors as we seek to be a blessing to the entire ministry of Milldale Baptist Church.

"To God be the praise and glory for what He has done for and through the senior adults at Milldale!"

Rinda Richards Davis[59]

"I can still remember my first trip to Milldale as a nine-year-old child, wondering where in the world we were going and when would we get there. We arrived at an old house where a small group of people were gathering. To a child very accustomed to traditional Baptist churches, this was an unusual experience. Our daily lives changed in ways we could not have imagined. It opened up a world of people that we would not have otherwise known and loved. My father is the late Collyn Richards, and my mother, all know as "Sue". They provided me the gift of coming to Milldale and all the spiritual background that came with it.

---

[59] Secretary, Milldale Baptist Church

The Milldale Story

"I can only attribute any spiritual knowledge that I possess to, first of all, the Holy Spirit's guidance, and secondly to the Bible Conference preaching of Dr. and Mrs. Stewart, all the way to the encouragement of Brother Ron Dunn and everyone in between. Words cannot describe this kind of spiritual education, free to us for all these years, provided by Brother Jimmy and a handful of people who obeyed God.

"As God in His providence has always seen fit to alter my life, I now am secretary for Milldale Baptist Church. Brother Danny and Nancy have been personal friends of my family for many years, and I look forward to the Lord's using us together in His work. Thank you, Milldale, for all you have done and all that you will do until the coming of our Lord!"

Bill Britt[60]

"I was first introduced to the ministry of Milldale Baptist Church and to Pastor Jimmy Robertson while I was a student at Louisiana College in Pineville, Louisiana. It was evident from the first visit on the grounds that it was a special place, and God's hand was on the ministry of Milldale. Bro. Jimmy has seen the vision that God gave him well over forty years ago come to fruition and touch the lives of tens of thousands around the world. From the ministry of the printed word, to camp meetings, to student camps; all of it has had the wind of Heaven blowing upon it! It has been over thirty years since my first visit, and all subsequent experiences have been priceless. Bro. Jimmy and many of the men who have preached at Milldale have become my heroes and mentors.

"Bro. Jimmy has allowed me the privilege and honor of preaching in many conferences through these years. It has been humbling, to say the least, to stand in the pulpit where some of the greatest men of God have stood to proclaim the Word of

---

[60] Evangelist, Gallatin, Tennessee. Also see testimony on page 81.

God. I have spent as many as four weeks out of the year, for many years, involved in conferences and camps. Many of the friendships that have been established there have been life changing for me. Bro. Jimmy, has not only taught the faith life, but has modeled it through all these years for me and scores of others."

Bill Sturm[61]

"I count it an honor and privilege to have been asked to write a testimony of what the Milldale Bible Conferences, the *Fires of Revival* paper, Brother Jimmy Robertson and others of the Milldale ministry have meant to me in my personal life and the life of my family.

"I started pastoring in Oklahoma in my early twenties, and it was during this period that I would receive the *Fires of Revival* paper. I would read every word of every article, and it was through the *"Fires"* paper that I became acquainted with some preachers who have had a tremendous impact on my ministry as a young pastor and later full-time evangelist. And how we are blessed to have someone like Mrs. Judy Scoggins who puts each of the *Fires of Revival* publications together and helps coordinate other aspects of the ministry.

"Because of the ministry of Milldale Baptist Church I came to know Brother Manley Beasley. I learned what it meant to walk by faith by watching his life. I have no idea where I would be today had I not learned the principles he taught.

"I also got to know Ron Dunn and also had the privilege of preaching with him. I listen to his tapes on *Chained to the Chariot* at least once a month. From him I learned what it meant for Jesus to be Lord of my life.

"I met Bro. Sonny Holland at Milldale, and from him I learned the vital importance of the consistent, steadfast walk with the Lord. I have watched him be faithful to preach in all sizes of churches. When God leads him to an overseas mission

---

[61] Evangelist, Valdosta, Georgia

field, he goes with no hesitation. He has been found faithful in his walk with the Lord day by day and moment by moment.

Larry Jordan[62]

"As a young pastor in the mid 1970's, I began receiving the *Fires of Revival* newspaper. The messages blessed my life and ministry. I filed many of these papers and still have them to this day. I dreamed of the day that I might get to go to a Milldale camp meeting and meet the founder, Bro. Jimmy Robertson. Little did I dream that I would one day have the honor and privilege to preach on a regular basis at the camp.

"Bro. Jimmy Robertson is a pastor's pastor. God has used him and the camp meetings to greatly influence and impact many pastors' lives and ministries. He has certainly been a tremendous encouragement and role model to me. He is a great man of faith and prayer, who has a heart for revival. Bro. Jimmy has always had the time for me and others, and his wife, Frances, has been a great role model to many pastors' wives. She has been a special blessing and encouragement to my wife, Donna.

"When I was in the pastorate, we took many people from our church to the Milldale Bible Camps. We have heard some of the greatest preachers in the world, the heroes of the faith. When you drive onto the grounds, you feel the very presence, power, and glory of God. Many pastors have come to the Camp ready to throw in the towel, but have left renewed, empowered by the Holy Spirit, and encouraged to finish strong. These camp meetings have truly been *"times of refreshing from the presence of the Lord."*

"Not only has Bro. Jimmy been a blessing to my life, but I have also grown to love and appreciate Danny Greig, Co-Camp

---

[62] Evangelist, Sulphur Springs, Texas

Appendix Two: In Their Own Words

Director, and Sonny Holland, Evangelist. They are men of God, full of His love, and they are a blessing to my life.

"Finally, I want to thank the Lord for raising up a Jimmy Robertson who obeyed Him and was used to start Milldale Bible Camp almost 50 years ago."

Willie Kennedy[63]

"I was providentially led to Milldale in the midst of my very first pastorate near Hammond, Louisiana. I read the *Fires of Revival* newspaper and felt I needed to attend the upcoming February, 1970, Camp Meeting. That meeting would change the course of my life and ministry.

"I'm reminded of Paul's question in Hebrews 11:32, when he was trying to mention all that came to mind when recalling the roll-call of faith, '*...and what shall I more say? For time would fail me to tell of....*' Somewhere in the continuing records and roll-call of the faithful, Milldale and Bro. Jimmy Robertson will be found written down.

"I could write a book about what God has done in my life in the subsequent years and even down to the present time through the ministry of Milldale. The Word of God, prayer, preaching, teaching, missions, and revival have always been predominate at Milldale, and I know it has continued that way largely through the godly influence of Bro. Jimmy. Over the years, he has been a role model and spiritual blessing to me.

"Bro. Jimmy, thank you so much for what you and Milldale have meant to my wife, Arlene, and me, to Faith Church, and to the radio ministry of *Sound Radio!* We're praying that God's grace and peace will be multiplied to you and Frances, and all at Milldale through our LORD and Savior, Jesus Christ!"

---

[63] Willie Kennedy, pastor of Faith Baptist Church and Faith Academy, Erwinville, Louisiana. Founder and president of "Sound Radio."

The Milldale Story

Ed and Billie Smith[64]

"Jimmy Robertson has been instrumental throughout our ministry. He preached many times at the 112 Revival Center. We have shared so many great times of fellowship. We have laughed together, prayed together, and cried together.

"I am proud to say that over the years, Billie and I have been blessed to be able to attend many conferences hosted by Milldale Baptist Church. Because of Jimmy Robertson's faithfulness, we have had the honor of hearing great men of God expound the Word of God.

"As we reflect back on our friendship with Jimmy Robertson, we consider him our mentor. He has taught us the walk of faith. Jimmy and Frances have been dear friends, and we will always be grateful for their sacrificial giving of their time, money, and words of encouragement."

Gordon McDaniel[65]

"In 1967, we were members of a church in Decatur, Georgia. Our pastor was acquainted with Milldale, so he organized a church trip to the summer Bible Conference. We left the church on Sunday night after the evening service in a convoy of three Volkswagon busses and four or five cars. When we arrived the next morning, there was the immediate evidence of the presence of God on the grounds.

---

[64] Ed and Billie Smith have been associated with Milldale since its inception. Ed pastored several churches, directed the 112 Revival Center, the Mizpash Home for Boys, and a Rescue Mission. The Smiths now have a retreat center in Haughton, Louisiana.

[65] In 1972, Jimmy Robertson resigned the pastorate of Milldale Baptist Church for a year during which time he directed the camps, the literature ministry, and preached the message of revival around the country. The church called Gordon McDaniel as pastor until Bro. Jimmy returned a year later.

Appendix Two: In Their Own Words

"One of the stand-out memories of this time did not take place in the meetings themselves, but in the dining hall. Meals were served family-style, and often, after a time of prayer, there would be a spontaneous outbreak of singing such as I had never experienced before.

"We left after the final evening service and headed back to Georgia. The theme of the meeting had been, *The Victorious Christian Life* or *The Sufficiency of Christ,* and we soon got to test this first hand, in the middle of the night. The motor on the bus I was driving burned up near Columbus, Mississippi, and we had to distribute all the passengers and luggage to other vehicles. But in spite of this inconvenience, we found that we were still able to rejoice in the Lord.

Called to Preach

"Because of the impact of that Milldale Camp Meeting, Juanita and I returned for the Thanksgiving Conference later that year, and as I look back, I can see that the seed being planted during those meetings resulted in my being called to preach the gospel in January, 1968; then, in the summer of 1969, our family, and the family of John Baker, went to one of the conferences a week early to assist in getting things ready.

Two things stand out about that meeting. The first is that Dr. James Stewart was there, and prior to the meeting he came up to me and said that he had been told I had been called to preach. He then led me to his book table at the rear of the tabernacle and began to gather a large stack of books to give me and Bro. Baker. I think we each got 25 to 30 of these items. Although the literature was a blessing, the greatest blessing was to have Dr. Stewart interested in our lives. I will never forget it.

"I was later called to pastor a church in Louisiana, then, after a couple of years of pastoring, I moved to Milldale and became involved in many aspects of the ministry. Although the conferences were greatly blessed, at that particular time the church was going through a struggle, and in 1972, I became its pastor for one year.

At the end of that year, when Bro. Jimmy returned, we moved away and were not closely associated with Milldale until in 1986, when we returned for the Thanksgiving conference. I was asked to preach one afternoon, and I prayed that the Lord would quicken His Word and quicken the people. We went away from that meeting renewed and refreshed, and it was not long before we felt the Lord leading us to move back to Milldale where we ended up staying for the next fifteen years.

"The ministry of this special place would not be complete without the many men who have played a significant part in the work and who have gone on to be with the Lord. I have such fond memories of Curtis McCarley, Duncan Campbell, Arthur Blackburn, James A. Stewart, Hyman Appleman, Harold Brown, Jessie Norris, Manley Beasley, Ron Dunn, Joe Parsons, Mel McClellan, Joe Prather, and others. Some not only ministered in a significant way, but became personal friends.

"Finally, a word about Milldale's pastor and camp director. You may be aware that Jimmy Robertson is not the ordinary traditional pastor, but over the years he has been a great friend and tremendous supporter. During our time at Milldale we went through some severe personal problems, but we could always count on Bro. Jimmy, day or night, to stand with us. Bro. Jimmy also went through some severe testings, and in some small way we have been able to stand with him.

"People attending the conferences over the years often leave thinking that Milldale must surely be a heaven on earth. Well, we all know that there is no perfect place here on earth, but the reality at Milldale is that, through the problems and the pressures, there have always been the praises and the blessings."

Appendix Two: In Their Own Words

Debbie Beasley[66]

"I remember Milldale as both a serious and a fun place. During the six years we lived there, I got to meet some of the greatest preachers and most godly men and women alive at that time. Just being around people like Jimmy Robertson, Sonny Holland, Duncan Campbell, James Alexander Stewart and his wife Ruth, Oswald J. Smith, who used to bring his son Paul with him, Jesse Norris, Bertha Smith, C. L. Culpepper, and Leonard Ravenhill, couldn't help but impact me as a young person growing up.

"There were a lot of us kids at Milldale. Milldale was a safe place to be, and we spent a lot of our time either riding the lawn mowers or riding horses. My Dad loved horses, and he got me interested in them. I ended up breeding and riding competitively.

"I thank God for the years I spent at Milldale, and as I look back, I realize how much they had to do with what I believe and the person I have become."

Iva May[67]

"Nothing about Milldale Baptist Church and its International ministry was typical. Working at the church's print shop brought the world to the door of my heart, and Milldale's revival camp meetings exposed me to the teachings of great men of God such as Manley Beasley, Jimmy Robertson, Roy Hession and others. Sitting under such preaching meant that I could not live the 'typical' Baptist existence. It was there that I first sensed God's call to full time Christian service. My missions' journey began in Israel, moved to Africa, then back to the States as a pastor and seminary professor's wife."

---

[66] Fayetteville, Arkansas. See also testimony in Chapter 26.
[67] Germantown, Tennessee. Author, conference speaker, and wife of Dr. Stan May, pastor and Mid America Seminary professor.

Mackey Willis[68]

"I first came to Milldale in 1979. I thought I had been saved when I was a young boy, but after hearing the Word of God preached at Milldale, I knew I was lost. I knelt at the altar and gave my heart to Jesus, and I have never been the same again. God began to do a work in my life, and I have attended Milldale every chance I can.

"At one of these conferences, Brother Ron Dunn was preaching on faith. He made a statement that helped me to understand the concept of faith as I had never understood it before. He said, 'Faith is the human response to a divine revelation.' That hit me, and I fully understood that if God tells me to do something, then I must act on it, and then I have acted in faith. But I must get the word from God first.

"Right after that message, they took an offering up. The Lord spoke to my heart and told me to give all that I had. I wanted to argue because I only had ten dollars left to get home on. God didn't argue. He just simply told me that one time to give all. When the plate passed I gave all I had, while, in my mind wondering how I was supposed to get home. As we left the service to go and eat in the dining hall, Jimmy Talley, a preacher friend, walked up to me, shook my hand and said, *"God told me to find you and give you this."* He handed me fifty dollars. God had spoken, I obeyed, and He met my need above what I ever would have known.

"Through the years God has shown Himself so faithful. I now travel in full-time evangelism and sing with my wife and son. God has blessed, and He has brought me back to Milldale for the past several years to sing at the Bible Conferences. I am truly blessed by God and by this place.

---

[68] The Mackey Willis Family, Music Evangelists, DeRidder, Louisiana

Indices

Index of Sermons

The Church God Will Use—47
God's Word—61
The Greatest Task—90
Where Does Revival Begin?—138
What is Faith? (part one)—153
What is Faith? (part two)—161
Take the Land!—188

Index of Testimonies

Jimmy Autin: 77
Debbie Beasley: 88, 207, 251
Manley Beasley, Jr.: 134
Marthé Beasley: 240
Bill Britt: 81, 244
Jackie Brown: 116
Ivan & Jackie Carlson: 103, 112
Mike Courtney: 63
Ken & Sharon Cummings: 117
Ronda Richards Davis: 243
Malcom Ellis: 69
Ken Fryer: 154
Tim & Rhonda Galipeau: 101
Danny Greig: 201-225
Janell Greig: 114
Nancy Greig: 233
Dorothy Holland: 229
Monte Holland: 51
Sonny Holland: 110, 118
Paul & Lolita Jones: 115

Larry Jordan: 246
Willie Kennedy: 247
Clinton & Viola Lee: 242
Iva May: 251
Gordon McDaniel: 248
Muriel Norris: 60, 238
Luther Price: 199
Frances Robertson: 227
Jason Robertson: 130
Philip Robertson: 32, 105, 123
Chuck Sackman: 47
Bill Scoggins: 56
Judy Scoggins: 53, 112
Ed & Billie Smith: 248
Jerry Spencer: 75, 78, 79, 149
Bill Sturm: 151, 220, 245
Elaine Talley: 147
Tribute to Jesse Norris: 169
Mackey Willis: 252

Index of Camp Meeting Preachers

Hyman Appleman
Rolfe Barnard
Manley Beasley
Manley Beasley Jr.
Henry Blackaby
Arthur Blackburn
Mickey Bonner
R. C. Branch
Paul Brand, MD
Bill Britt
Frank Boydstun
Paul Boughan
Harold Brown
C. S. Cadwalder
B.B. Caldwell
Duncan Campbell
Ivan Kerr
Carl Carrigan
Jerry Chaddick
Morris Chapman
Pete Charpentier
R.E. Clark
Harold Clayton
Jimmy Coleman
John Collier
James Courtney
Mike Courtney
Jim Cymbala
Charles Culpepper
Harold Danley
Gov. Jimmy Davis
Bob Doom
Bob Dollar
Kevin Dunn
Ron Dunn
Malcom Ellis

Perry Ellis
Vlado Fajfr
Ken Fryer
Al Gaspard
Bruce Gill
Ed Greig
Danny Greig
Jim Hill
Lawrence Haley
Roger Haney
Roy Hession
John Hilbun
Preston Holder
Sonny Holland
Phillip Hudson
Dave Hunt
Peter Hutchison
Randel Jackson
Fred Jarvis
Larry Jordan
Willie Kennedy
Jeff LaBorg
R. G. Lee
Danny Lovett
Lynn Martin
Milton Martin
Ed McAteer
Curtis McCarley
Mel McClellan
Caldwell McCoy
Gordon McDaniel
Wiley McGhee
John Merck
Jon Moore
Joe Murray
Conrad Murrell

Jesse Norris
Jerry Oliver
Joe Parsons
Bob Pitman
Harlan Popov
Joe Prather
Luther Price
Jeremy Pruitt
Leonard Ravenhill
Herb Reavis
Bill Riddick
Bill Robertson
Jimmy Robertson
Jason Robertson
Philip Robertson
James Robison
Avery Rogers
Jimmy Sasser
Jim Sheet
Russell Shelton
Sonny Simpson
J. Harold Smith
Oswald J. Smith
Ed Smith
Jerry Spencer
Dan Spencer
Bill Stafford
James A. Stewart
Bill Sturm
Larry Swift
Jimmy Talley
J. W. Taylor
Jack Taylor
Major Ian Thomas
Robert Toney
Keith Zachary
(and more)

# Photo Gallery

From 16 acres and a farm house in 1963
to a ministry that touched the world

Milldale dining room and tabernacle

State of Louisiana

M. J. "Mike" Foster, Jr.
Governor

Official Statement

WHEREAS, Reverend Jimmy Robertson has faithfully preached the gospel for 50 years; and

WHEREAS, thousands of lives around the world have been touched through the printing ministry of Milldale International Ministries; and

WHEREAS, the call for revival has been proclaimed through the publication of "Fires of Revival"; and

WHEREAS, the Milldale Bible Conferences and Summer Camps have impacted a vast number of Christians from around Louisiana and across the United States; and

WHEREAS, Jimmy Robertson has faithfully served as pastor of the Milldale Baptist Church for the past 37 years.

NOW, THEREFORE, I, M.J. "Mike" Foster, Jr., Governor of the state of Louisiana, do hereby commend

REVEREND JIMMY ROBERTSON

In Witness Whereof, I have hereunto set my hand officially and caused to be affixed the Executive Seal of the State of Louisiana, at the Capitol, in the City of Baton Rouge, on this the ___7th___ day of ___February___ A.D., ___2001___

Governor of Louisiana

The Robertson children. Jimmy seated front left

Jimmy with Bob Holland, contractor who built the early Milldale buildings

Jimmy, age 19, preaching on the bank of the Tickfaw River

Bro. Jimmy and Frances—50th wedding anniversary

Ruth and James A. Stewart

Ron and Kaye Dunn (center) with Bill and Sue Stafford

Jimmy Robertson, James Stewart, Sonny Holland, Manley Beasley

James A Stewart and R.G. Lee   Oswald J. Smith

Burning of the Milldale note, 1968. Bro. Jimmy at podium
Louis Robertson, Lynda & Henry Sibley, Ray Robertson, Danny Greig

Judy Scoggins, Jimmy & Frances Robertson

Ivan Carlson and the King Press   Jackie Carlson, multi-tasking

Shipment destined for an Iron Curtain country

Jimmy and Frances with their children and spouses
Cathy & Dwayne Buhler, James Robertson, Keith & Kim
Robertson

Danny and Nancy Greig with sons Matthew and Michael

Seated: Louis Robertson, Opel (Mom) Hudson, Frances
Robertson
Standing: Philip and Zack Hudson, Jimmy Robertson

Front: J.W. Taylor, Jimmy Robertson, Joe Prather
Back: Kenneth Wall, Harold Brown, Danny Greig

Jimmy Robertson, Jessie Norris and Sonny Holland

Front: Janell Greig and Muriel Norris
Back: Frances Robertson and Dorothy Holland

Please—you first!
Bro. Jimmy, Sonny, Ron Owens and Henry Blackaby

Milldale food—for the body as well as soul and spirit

Ed Robertson, Chef

Sonny and Dorothy Holland, Jimmy and Frances Robertson, Nancy and Danny Greig

Danny, Sonny and Bro. Jimmy

Jeff and Charity Phillips, Milldale ministry associates With Danny and Nancy Greig

Contact Information

Milldale Baptist Church
11950 Milldale Road
Zachary, LA 70791

Telephone: 225-654-8168
or   225-654-5065

Email
milldale@milldalebaptistchurch.org

Website
www.milldalebaptistchurch.org

Comments welcome
Judy Scoggins: judyfor@rof.net
Ron Owens: ronowens3@gmail.com

Other books by Ron Owens
They Could Not Stop the Music
Return to Worship
Worship: Believers Experiencing God
(co-authored with Henry Blackaby)
Manley Beasley: Man of Faith, Instrument of Revival
Iris: Trophy of Grace
Call Me Blue
Ron Dunn: His Life and Mission

www.ingramcontent.com/pod-product-compliance
Lightning Source LLC
Chambersburg PA
CBHW060114170426
43198CB00010B/894